Brander Matthews

Poems of American Patriotism

Brander Matthews

Poems of American Partriotism

ISBN/EAN: 9783744771269

Printed in Europe, USA, Canada, Australia, Japan

Cover: Foto ©Thomas Meinert / pixelio.de

More available books at **www.hansebooks.com**

POEMS

OF

AMERICAN PATRIOTISM.

POEMS

OF

AMERICAN PATRIOTISM

CHOSEN BY

(J.) BRANDER MATTHEWS

NEW-YORK
CHARLES SCRIBNER'S SONS
1882

Who now shall sneer?
Who dare again to say we trace
Our lines to a plebeian race?
Roundhead and Cavalier!
Dumb are those names, erewhile in battle loud;
Dream-footed, as the shadow of a cloud,
They flit across the ear;
That is best blood that hath most iron in 't
To edge resolve with, pouring without stint
For what makes manhood dear.
Tell us not of Plantagenets,
Hapsburgs, and Guelphs, whose thin bloods crawl
Down from some victor in a border brawl!
· How poor their outworn coronets,
Matched with one leaf of that plain civic wreath
Our brave for honor's blazon shall bequeath,
Through whose desert a rescued Nation sets
Her heel on treason, and the trumpet hears
Shout victory, tingling Europe's sullen ears
With vain resentments and more vain regrets!

JAMES RUSSELL LOWELL.

PREFATORY NOTE.

An attempt has been made in the present collection to gather together the patriotic poems of America, those which depict feelings as well as those which describe actions, since these latter are as indicative of the temper of the time. It is a collection, for the most part, of old favorites, for Americans have been quick to take to heart a stirring telling of a daring and noble deed; but these may be found to have gained freshness by a grouping in order. The arrangement is chronological so far as it might be, that the history of America as told by her poets should be set forth. Here and there occur breaks in the story, chiefly because there are fit incidents for song which no poet has fitly sung as yet.

The poems have been printed scrupulously from the best accessible text, and they have not been tinkered in any way, though some few have been curtailed slightly for the sake of space. In a few cases, where the whole poem has not fallen within the scope of this volume, only a fragment is here given. When this has been done, it is pointed out. Brief notes have been prefixed to many of the poems, making plain the occasion of their origin, and removing any chance obscurity of allusion.

The editor takes pleasure in expressing his thanks to the friends who have aided him, and especially to Mr. Henry Gallup Paine, who has given invaluable help in research and in the correction of the text. He desires also to acknowledge his indebtedness to the authors who have kindly answered his appeals, and to the publishers who have given permission to make use of copyright matter. To Messrs. Houghton, Mifflin & Co. in particular are his obligations heavy, since his task would have been hopeless had they denied him the privilege of borrowing from the works of the many American poets for whom they publish.

J. B. M.

New-York, November, 1882.

TABLE OF CONTENTS.

BOSTON.

SICUT PATRIBUS, SIT DEUS NOBIS.

Dec. 16,
1773.

*This poem was read in Faneuil Hall, on the Centen-
nial Anniversary of the "Boston Tea-party," at
which a band of men disguised as Indians had
quietly emptied into the sea the taxed tea-chests of
three British ships.*

THE rocky nook with hill-tops three
　　Looked eastward from the farms,
And twice each day the flowing sea
　　Took Boston in its arms;
　　　　The men of yore were stout and poor,
　　　　And sailed for bread to every shore.

And where they went on trade intent
　　They did what freemen can,
Their dauntless ways did all men praise,
　　The merchant was a man.
　　　　The world was made for honest trade,—
　　　　To plant and eat be none afraid.

The waves that rocked them on the deep
　To them their secret told;
Said the winds that sung the lads to sleep,
　" Like us be free and bold ! "
　　　The honest waves refuse to slaves
　　　The empire of the ocean caves.

Old Europe groans with palaces,
　Has lords enough and more;—
We plant and build by foaming seas
　A city of the poor;—
　　　For day by day could Boston Bay
　　　Their honest labor overpay.

We grant no dukedoms to the few,
　We hold like rights and shall;—
Equal on Sunday in the pew,
　On Monday in the mall.
　　　For what avail the plough or sail,
　　　Or land or life, if freedom fail?

The noble craftsmen we promote,
 Disown the knave and fool;
Each honest man shall have his vote,
 Each child shall have his school.
  A union then of honest men,
  Or union nevermore again.

The wild rose and the barberry thorn
 Hung out their summer pride
Where now on heated pavements worn
 The feet of millions stride.

Fair rose the planted hills behind
 The good town on the bay,
And where the western hills declined
 The prairie stretched away.

What care though rival cities soar
 Along the stormy coast:

Penn's town, New York, and Baltimore,
   If Boston knew the most!

They laughed to know the world so wide;
   The mountains said: "Good-day!
We greet you well, you Saxon men,
   Up with your towns and stay!"
      The world was made for honest trade,—
      To plant and eat be none afraid.

"For you," they said, "no barriers be,
   For you no sluggard rest;
Each street leads downward to the sea,
   Or landward to the West."

O happy town beside the sea,
   Whose roads lead everywhere to all;
Than thine no deeper moat can be,
   No stouter fence, no steeper wall!

Bad news from George on the English throne:
   "You are thriving well," said he;

" Now by these presents be it known,
    You shall pay us a tax on tea ;
      'T is very small, — no load at all, —
      Honor enough that we send the call."

" Not so," said Boston, "good my lord,
    We pay your governors here
Abundant for their bed and board,
    Six thousand pounds a year.
(Your highness knows our homely word,)
      Millions for self-government,
      But for tribute never a cent."

The cargo came ! and who could blame
    If *Indians* seized the tea,
And, chest by chest, let down the same
    Into the laughing sea ?
      For what avail the plough or sail
      Or land or life, if freedom fail ?

The townsmen braved the English king,
    Found friendship in the French,

And Honor joined the patriot ring
  Low on their wooden bench.

O bounteous seas that never fail!
  O day remembered yet!
O happy port that spied the sail
  Which wafted Lafayette!
      Pole-star of light in Europe's night,
      That never faltered from the right.

Kings shook with fear, old empires crave
  The secret force to find
Which fired the little State to save
  The rights of all mankind.

But right is might through all the world;
  Province to province faithful clung,
Through good and ill the war-bolt hurled,
  Till Freedom cheered and the joy-bells rung.

The sea returning day by day
  Restores the world-wide mart;

BOSTON.

So let each dweller on the Bay
  Fold Boston in his heart,
      Till these echoes be choked with snows,
      Or over the town blue ocean flows.

Let the blood of her hundred thousands
  Throb in each manly vein;
And the wit of all her wisest,
  Make sunshine in her brain.
      For you can teach the lightning speech,
      And round the globe your voices reach.

And each shall care for other,
  And each to each shall bend,
To the poor a noble brother,
  To the good an equal friend.

A blessing through the ages thus
  Shield all thy roofs and towers!
God with the fathers, so with us,
  Thou darling town of ours!

                    RALPH WALDO EMERSON.

PAUL REVERE'S RIDE.

April 18,
1775.

*This poem is the "Landlord's Tale," the first of the
"Tales of a Wayside Inn."*

LISTEN, my children, and you shall hear
Of the midnight ride of Paul Revere,
On the eighteenth of April, in Seventy-Five:
Hardly a man is now alive
Who remembers that famous day and year.

He said to his friend, "If the British march
By land or sea from the town to-night,
Hang a lantern aloft in the belfry arch
Of the North Church tower as a signal-light,
One, if by land, and two, if by sea;
And I on the opposite shore will be,
Ready to ride and spread the alarm
Through every Middlesex village and farm,
For the country folk to be up and to arm."

Then he said, Good night! and with muffled oar
Silently rowed to the Charlestown shore,
Just as the moon rose over the bay,
Where swinging wide at her moorings lay
The Somerset, British man-of-war;
A phantom ship, with each mast and spar
Across the moon like a prison-bar,
And a huge black hulk, that was magnified
By its own reflection in the tide.

Meanwhile, his friend, through alley and street
Wanders and watches with eager ears,
Till in the silence around him he hears
The muster of men at the barrack door,
The sound of arms, and the tramp of feet,
And the measured tread of the grenadiers,
Marching down to their boats on the shore.

Then he climbed to the tower of the Old North Church,
By the wooden stairs, with stealthy tread,

To the belfry-chamber overhead,
And startled the pigeons from their perch
On the sombre rafters, that round him made
Masses and moving shapes of shade,—
By the trembling ladder, steep and tall,
To the highest window in the wall,
Where he paused to listen and look down
A moment on the roofs of the town,
And the moonlight flowing over all.

Beneath, in the churchyard, lay the dead,
In their night-encampment on the hill,
Wrapped in silence so deep and still
That he could hear, like a sentinel's tread,
The watchful night-wind, as it went
Creeping along from tent to tent,
And seeming to whisper, "All is well!"
A moment only he feels the spell
Of the place and the hour, and the secret dread
Of the lonely belfry and the dead;
For suddenly all his thoughts are bent

On a shadowy something far away,
Where the river widens to meet the bay,—
A line of black that bends and floats
On the rising tide, like a bridge of boats.

Meanwhile, impatient to mount and ride,
Booted and spurred, with a heavy stride
On the opposite shore walked Paul Revere.
Now he patted his horse's side,
Now gazed at the landscape far and near,
Then, impetuous, stamped the earth,
And turned and tightened his saddle-girth;
But mostly he watched with eager search
The belfry-tower of the Old North Church,
As it rose above the graves on the hill,
Lonely, and spectral, and sombre and still.
And lo! as he looks, on the belfry's height
A glimmer, and then a gleam of light!
He springs to the saddle, the bridle he turns,
But lingers and gazes, till full on his sight
A second lamp in the belfry burns!

A hurry of hoofs in a village street,
A shape in the moonlight, a bulk in the dark,
And beneath, from the pebbles, in passing, a spark
Struck out by a steed flying fearless and fleet:
That was all! And yet, through the gloom and the light,
The fate of a nation was riding that night;
And the spark struck out by that steed, in his flight,
Kindled the land into flame with its heat.

He has left the village and mounted the steep,
And beneath him, tranquil and broad and deep,
Is the Mystic, meeting the ocean tides;
And under the alders, that skirt its edge,
Now soft on the sand, now loud on the ledge,
Is heard the tramp of his steed as he rides.

It was twelve by the village clock
When he crossed the bridge into Medford town.
He heard the crowing of the cock,
And the barking of the farmer's dog,

And felt the damp of the river fog,
That rises after the sun goes down.

It was one by the village clock,
When he rode into Lexington.
He saw the gilded weathercock
Swim in the moonlight as he passed,
And the meeting-house windows, blank and bare,
Gaze at him with a spectral glare,
As if they already stood aghast
At the bloody work they would look upon.

It was two by the village clock,
When he came to the bridge in Concord town.
He heard the bleating of the flock,
And the twitter of birds among the trees,
And felt the breath of the morning breeze
Blowing over the meadows brown.
And one was safe and asleep in his bed
Who at the bridge would be first to fall,
Who that day would be lying dead,
Pierced by a British musket-ball.

You know the rest. In the books you have read,
How the British Regulars fired and fled,—
How the farmers gave them ball for ball,
From behind each fence and farm-yard wall,
Chasing the red-coats down the lane,
Then crossing the fields to emerge again
Under the trees at the turn of the road,
And only pausing to fire and load.

So through the night rode Paul Revere;
And so through the night went his cry of alarm
To every Middlesex village and farm,—
A cry of defiance and not of fear,
A voice in the darkness, a knock at the door,
And a word that shall echo forevermore!
For, borne on the night-wind of the Past,
Through all our history, to the last,
In the hour of darkness and peril and need,
The people will waken and listen to hear
The hurrying hoof-beats of that steed,
And the midnight message of Paul Revere.

HENRY WADSWORTH LONGFELLOW.

THE BATTLE OF LEXINGTON.

April 19, 1775.

The skirmish at Lexington and the fight at Concord closed all political bickering between Great Britain and her colonies and began the War of the Revolution. The following verses are a fragment of the " Psalm of the West."

THEN haste ye, Prescott and Revere!
  Bring all the men of Lincoln here;
Let Chelmsford, Littleton, Carlisle,
Let Acton, Bedford, hither file —
Oh, hither file, and plainly see
Out of a wound leap Liberty.

Say, Woodman April! all in green,
Say, Robin April! hast thou seen
In all thy travel round the earth
Ever a morn of calmer birth?
But Morning's eye alone serene
Can gaze across yon village-green
To where the trooping British run
    Through Lexington.

Good men in fustian, stand ye still;
The men in red come o'er the hill,
Lay down your arms, damned rebels! cry
The men in red full haughtily.
But never a grounding gun is heard;
The men in fustian stand unstirred;
Dead calm, save maybe a wise bluebird
Puts in his little heavenly word.
O men in red! if ye but knew
The half as much as bluebirds do,
Now in this little tender calm
Each hand would out, and every palm
With patriot palm strike brotherhood's stroke
Or ere these lines of battle broke.

O men in red! if ye but knew
The least of all that bluebirds do,
Now in this little godly calm
Yon voice might sing the Future's Psalm —
The Psalm of Love with the brotherly eyes
Who pardons and is very wise —

Yon voice that shouts, high-hoarse with ire,
    Fire !

The red-coats fire, the homespuns fall:
The homespuns' anxious voices call,
Brother, art hurt ? and *Where hit, John ?*
And, *Wipe this blood,* and *Men, come on,*
And *Neighbor, do but lift my head,*
And *Who is wounded ?   Who is dead ?*
Seven are killed.   My God !   my God !
Seven lie dead on the village sod.
Two Harringtons, Parker, Hadley, Brown,
Monroe and Porter,— these are down.
Nay, look ! stout Harrington not yet dead !
He crooks his elbow, lifts his head.
He lies at the step of his own house-door;
He crawls and makes a path of gore.
The wife from the window hath seen, and rushed;
He hath reached the step, but the blood hath gushed;
He hath crawled to the step of his own house-door,
But his head hath dropped: he will crawl no more.

2

Clasp, Wife, and kiss, and lift the head:
Harrington lies at his doorstep dead.

But, O ye Six that round him lay
And bloodied up that April day!
As Harrington fell, ye likewise fell —
At the door of the House wherein ye dwell;
As Harrington came, ye likewise came
And died at the door of your House of Fame.

SIDNEY LANIER.

HYMN.

April 19, 1775.

This poem was written to be sung at the completion of the Concord Monument, April 19, 1836.

BY the rude bridge that arched the flood,
   Their flag to April's breeze unfurled,
Here once the embattled farmers stood,
   And fired the shot heard round the world.

The foe long since in silence slept;
   Alike the conqueror silent sleeps;
And Time the ruined bridge has swept
   Down the dark stream which seaward creeps.

On this green bank, by this soft stream,
   We set to-day a votive stone;
That memory may their deed redeem,
   When, like our sires, our sons are gone.

19

HYMN.

Spirit, that made those heroes dare
  To die, or leave their children free,
Bid Time and Nature gently spare
  The shaft we raise to them and thee.

RALPH WALDO EMERSON.

TICONDEROGA.

May 10, 1775.

*After the news of Concord fight, a volunteer expedition
from Vermont and Connecticut, under Ethan Allen
and Benedict Arnold, seized Ticonderoga and Crown
Point, whose military stores were of great service.
From its chime of bells, the French called Ticonderoga
"Carillon."*

THE cold, gray light of the dawning
    On old Carillon falls,
And dim in the mist of the morning
    Stand the grim old fortress walls.
No sound disturbs the stillness
    Save the cataract's mellow roar,
Silent as death is the fortress,
    Silent the misty shore.

But up from the wakening waters
    Comes the cool, fresh morning breeze,
Lifting the banner of Britain,
    And whispering to the trees

Of the swift gliding boats on the waters
  That are nearing the fog-shrouded land,
With the old Green Mountain Lion,
  And his daring patriot band.

But the sentinel at the postern
  Heard not the whisper low;
He is dreaming of the banks of the Shannon
  As he walks on his beat to and fro,
Of the starry eyes in Green Erin
  That were dim when he marched away,
And a tear down his bronzed cheek courses,
  'T is the first for many a day.

A sound breaks the misty stillness,
  And quickly he glances around;
Through the mist, forms like towering giants
  Seem rising out of the ground;
A challenge, the firelock flashes,
  A sword cleaves the quivering air,
And the sentry lies dead by the postern,
  Blood staining his bright yellow hair.

Then, with a shout that awakens
   All the echoes of hillside and glen,
Through the low, frowning gate of the fortress,
   Sword in hand, rush the Green Mountain men.
The scarce wakened troops of the garrison
   Yield up their trust pale with fear;
And down comes the bright British banner,
   And out rings a Green Mountain cheer.

Flushed with pride, the whole eastern heavens
   With crimson and gold are ablaze;
And up springs the sun in his splendor
   And flings down his arrowy rays,
Bathing in sunlight the fortress,
   Turning to gold the grim walls,
While louder and clearer and higher
   Rings the song of the waterfalls.

Since the taking of Ticonderoga
   A century has rolled away;
But with pride the nation remembers
   That glorious morning in May.

And the cataract's silvery music
Forever the story tells,
Of the capture of old Carillon,
The chime of the silver bells.

V. B. WILSON.

GRANDMOTHER'S STORY OF BUNKER HILL BATTLE.

As she saw it from the Belfry.

June 17,
1775.

'TIS like stirring living embers when, at eighty,
one remembers
All the achings and the quakings of "the times that
tried men's souls";
When I talk of *Whig* and *Tory*, when I tell the *Rebel*
story,
To you the words are ashes, but to me they 're burning coals.

I had heard the muskets' rattle of the April running
battle;
Lord Percy's hunted soldiers, I can see their red coats
still;

But a deadly chill comes o'er me, as the day looms up
before me,
When a thousand men lay bleeding on the slopes of
Bunker's Hill.

'T was a peaceful summer's morning, when the first
thing gave us warning
Was the booming of the cannon from the river and the
shore:
" Child," says grandma, " what 's the matter, what is
all this noise and clatter?
Have those scalping Indian devils come to murder us
once more?"

Poor old soul! my sides were shaking in the midst of
all my quaking
To hear her talk of Indians when the guns began to
roar:
She had seen the burning village, and the slaughter and
the pillage,
When the Mohawks killed her father, with their bullets
through his door.

Then I said, " Now, dear old granny, don't you fret
and worry any,

For I 'll soon come back and tell you whether this is
work or play;

There can't be mischief in it, so I won't be gone a
minute " —

For a minute then I started. I was gone the livelong
day.

No time for bodice-lacing or for looking-glass grimacing;

Down my hair went as I hurried, tumbling half-way to
my heels;

God forbid your ever knowing, when there 's blood
around her flowing,

How the lonely, helpless daughter of a quiet household
feels!

In the street I heard a thumping; and I knew it was
the stumping

Of the Corporal, our old neighbor, on that wooden leg
he wore,

With a knot of women round him, — it was lucky I had
    found him, —
So I followed with the others, and the Corporal marched
    before.

They were making for the steeple, — the old soldier and
    his people;
The pigeons circled round us as we climbed the creak-
    ing stair,
Just across the narrow river — O, so close it made me
    shiver! —
Stood a fortress on the hill-top that but yesterday was
    bare.

Not slow our eyes to find it; well we knew who stood
    behind it,
Though the earthwork hid them from us, and the
    stubborn walls were dumb:
Here were sister, wife, and mother, looking wild upon
    each other,
And their lips were white with terror as they said, THE
    HOUR HAS COME!

The morning slowly wasted, not a morsel had we
   tasted,
And our heads were almost splitting with the cannons'
   deafening thrill,
When a 'figure tall and stately round the rampart strode
   sedately;
It was PRESCOTT, one since told me; he commanded on
   the hill.

Every woman's heart grew bigger when we saw his
   manly figure,
With the banyan buckled round it, standing up so
   straight and tall;
Like a gentleman of leisure who is strolling out for
   pleasure,
Through the storm of shells and cannon-shot he walked
   around the wall.

At eleven the streets were swarming, for the red-coats'
   ranks were forming;
At noon in marching order they were moving to
   the piers;

How the bayonets gleamed and glistened, as we looked
   far down and listened
To the trampling and the drum-beat of the belted
   grenadiers!

At length the men have started, with a cheer (it seemed
   faint-hearted),
In their scarlet regimentals, with their knapsacks on
   their backs,
And the reddening, rippling water, as after a sea-fight's
   slaughter,
Round the barges gliding onward blushed like blood
   along their tracks.

So they crossed to the other border, and again they
   formed in order;
And the boats came back for soldiers, came for soldiers,
   soldiers still:
The time seemed everlasting to us women faint and
   fasting,—
At last they 're moving, marching, marching proudly
   up the hill.

We can see the bright steel glancing all along the lines
    advancing—

Now the front rank fires a volley — they have thrown
    away their shot;

For behind the earthwork lying, all the balls above
    them flying,

Our people need not hurry; so they wait and answer
    not.

Then the Corporal, our old cripple (he would swear
    sometimes and tipple),—

He had heard the bullets whistle (in the old French
    war) before,—

Calls out in words of jeering, just as if they all were
    hearing,—

And his wooden leg thumps fiercely on the dusty bel-
    fry floor:—

"Oh! fire away, ye villains, and earn King George's
    shillin's,

But ye 'll waste a ton of powder afore a 'rebel' falls ;

You may bang the dirt and welcome, they 're as safe
    as Dan'l Malcolm
Ten foot beneath the gravestone that you 've splin-
    tered with your balls!"

In the hush of expectation, in the awe and trepidation
Of the dread approaching moment, we are well-nigh
    breathless all;
Though the rotten bars are failing on the rickety bel-
    fry railing,
We are crowding up against them like the waves
    against a wall.

Just a glimpse (the air is clearer), they are nearer,—
    nearer,— nearer,
When a flash — a curling smoke-wreath — then a crash
    — the steeple shakes —
The deadly truce is ended; the tempest's shroud is
    rended;
Like a morning mist it gathered, like a thunder-cloud
    it breaks!

O the sight our eyes discover as the blue-black smoke
    blows over!
The red-coats stretched in windrows as a mower rakes
    his hay;
Here a scarlet heap is lying, there a headlong crowd is
    flying
Like a billow that has broken and is shivered into
    spray.

Then we cried, "The troops are routed! they are beat
    — it can't be doubted!
God be thanked, the fight is over!"— Ah! the grim
    old soldier's smile!
"Tell us, tell us why you look so?" (we could hardly
    speak, we shook so),—
"Are they beaten? *Are* they beaten? ARE they beat-
    en?"—"Wait a while."

O the trembling and the terror! for too soon we saw
    our error:
They are baffled, not defeated; we have driven them
    back in vain;

3

And the columns that were scattered, round the colors
that were tattered,
Toward the sullen silent fortress turn their belted
breasts again.

All at once, as we are gazing, lo the roofs of Charlestown blazing!
They have fired the harmless village; in an hour it
will be down!
The Lord in heaven confound them, rain his fire and
brimstone round them, —
The robbing, murdering red-coats, that would burn a
peaceful town!

They are marching, stern and solemn; we can see each
massive column
As they near the naked earth-mound with the slanting
walls so steep.
Have our soldiers got faint-hearted, and in noiseless
haste departed?
Are they panic-struck and helpless? Are they palsied
or asleep?

Now! the walls they 're almost under! scarce a rod the
foes asunder!

Not a firelock flashed against them! up the earthwork
they will swarm!

But the words have scarce been spoken, when the
ominous calm is broken,

And a bellowing crash has emptied all the vengeance
of the storm!

So again, with murderous slaughter, pelted backward to
the water,

Fly Pigot's running heroes and the frightened braves
of Howe;

And we shout, "At last they 're done for, it 's their
barges they have run for:

They are beaten, beaten, beaten; and the battle 's
over now!"

And we looked, poor timid creatures, on the rough old
soldier's features,

Our lips afraid to question, but he knew what we would
ask:

"Not sure," he said; "keep quiet,— once more, I guess,
    they 'll try it —
Here 's damnation to the cut-throats!"—then he
    handed me his flask,

Saying, "Gal, you 're looking shaky; have a drop of
    old Jamaiky;
I 'm afraid there 'll be more trouble afore this job is
    done";
So I took one scorching swallow; dreadful faint I felt
    and hollow,
Standing there from early morning when the firing was
    begun.

All through those hours of trial I had watched a calm
    clock dial,
As the hands kept creeping, creeping,— they were creep-
    ing round to four,
When the old man said, "They 're forming with their
    bagonets fixed for storming:
It 's the death grip that's a coming,— they will try the
    works once more."

With brazen trumpets blaring, the flames behind them
    glaring,
The deadly wall before them, in close array they
    come;
Still onward, upward toiling, like a dragon's fold uncoil-
    ing —
Like the rattlesnake's shrill warning the reverberating
    drum !

Over heaps all torn and gory — shall I tell the fearful
    story,
How they surged above the breastwork, as a sea
    · breaks over a deck ;
How, driven, yet scarce defeated, our worn-out men re-
    treated,
With their powder-horns all emptied, like the swimmers
    from a wreck ?

It has all been told and painted ; as for me, they say
    I fainted,
And the wooden-legged old Corporal stumped with
    me down the stair :

When I woke from dreams affrighted the evening lamps
    were lighted,—
On the floor a youth was lying; his bleeding breast
    was bare.

And I heard through all the flurry, " Send for WARREN!
    hurry! hurry!
Tell him here 's a soldier bleeding, and he 'll come and
    dress his wound!"
Ah, we knew not till the morrow told its tale of death
    and sorrow,
How the starlight found him stiffened on the dark and
    bloody ground.

Who the youth was, what his name was, where the
    place from which he came was,
Who had brought him from the battle, and had left him
    at our door,
He could not speak to tell us; but 't was one of our
    brave fellows,
As the homespun plainly showed us which the dying
    soldier wore.

For they all thought he was dying, as they gathered
    'round him crying,—

And they said, " O, how they 'll miss him!" and,
    " What will his mother do ? "

Then, his eyelids just unclosing like a child's that has
    been dozing,

He faintly murmured, " Mother ! "——and—I saw his
    eyes were blue.

—" Why, grandma, how you 're winking ! "—Ah, my
    child, it sets me thinking

Of a story not like this one. Well, he somehow lived
    along;

So we came to know each other, and I nursed him
    like a—mother,

Till at last he stood before me, tall, and rosy-cheeked,
    and strong.

And we sometimes walked together in the pleasant
    summer weather ;

—" Please to tell us what his name was ? "—Just your
    own, my little dear,—

There 's his picture Copley painted : we became so
   well acquainted,
That—in short, that 's why I 'm grandma, and you
   children all are here !

OLIVER WENDELL HOLMES.

WARREN'S ADDRESS.

June 17, 1775,

Joseph Warren was commissioned by Massachusetts as a Major-General three days before the battle of Bunker Hill, at which he fought as a volunteer. He was one of the last to leave the field, and as a British officer in the redoubt called to him to surrender, a ball struck him in the forehead, killing him instantly.

STAND! the ground 's your own, my braves!
　　Will ye give it up to slaves?
Will ye look for greener graves?
　　　Hope ye mercy still?
What 's the mercy despots feel?
Hear it in that battle-peal!
Read it on yon bristling steel!
　　　Ask it,—ye who will.

Fear ye foes who kill for hire?
Will ye to your *homes* retire?
Look behind you! they 're a-fire!
　　　And, before you, see

Who have done it!—From the vale
On they come!—And will ye quail?—
Leaden rain and iron hail
    Let their welcome be!

In the God of battles trust!
Die we may,—and die we must;-
But, O, where can dust to dust
    Be consigned so well,
As where Heaven its dews shall shed
On the martyred patriot's bed,
And the rocks shall raise their head,
    Of his deeds to tell!

                      JOHN PIERPONT.

THE OLD CONTINENTALS.

1775–
1783.

*The nucleus of the Continental Army was the New
England force gathered before Boston, to the command of which Washington was appointed two days
before the battle of Bunker Hill, although he arrived too late to take part in that fight.*

IN their ragged regimentals
  Stood the old continentals,
    Yielding not,
When the grenadiers were lunging,
And like hail fell the plunging
    Cannon-shot;
    When the files
    Of the isles
From the smoky night encampment, bore the banner
      of the rampant
    Unicorn,
And grummer, grummer, grummer rolled the roll of
      the drummer,
    Through the morn!

43

Then with eyes to the front all,
And with guns horizontal,
  Stood our sires;
And the balls whistled deadly,
And in streams flashing redly
  Blazed the fires;
    As the roar
    On the shore,
Swept the strong battle-breakers o'er the green-sodded
      acres
    Of the plain;
And louder, louder, louder cracked the black gun-
      powder,
    Cracking amain!

Now like smiths at their forges
Worked the red St. George's
  Cannoneers;
And the " villainous saltpetre "
Rung a fierce, discordant metre
  Round their ears;
    As the swift

Storm-drift,

With hot sweeping anger, came the horse-guards'
clangor

On our flanks.

Then higher, higher, higher burned the old-fashioned fire

Through the ranks!

Then the old-fashioned colonel

Galloped through the white infernal

Powder-cloud;

And his broad-sword was swinging,

And his brazen throat was ringing

Trumpet loud.

Then the blue

Bullets flew,

And the trooper-jackets redden at the touch of the
leaden

Rifle-breath;

And rounder, rounder, rounder roared the iron six-
pounder,

Hurling death!

Guy Humphrey McMaster.

NATHAN HALE.

Sept. 22,
1776.

*After the retreat from Long Island, Washington needed
information as to the British strength. Captain
Nathan Hale, a young man of twenty-one, volun-
teered to get this. He was taken, inside the enemy's
lines, and hanged as a spy, regretting that he had
but one life to lose for his country.*

TO drum-beat and heart-beat,
  A soldier marches by:
There is color in his cheek,
  There is courage in his eye,
Yet to drum-beat and heart-beat
  In a moment he must die.

By starlight and moonlight,
  He seeks the Briton's camp;
He hears the rustling flag,
  And the armèd sentry's tramp;
And the starlight and moonlight
  His silent wanderings lamp.

46

With slow tread and still tread,
　　He scans the tented line;
And he counts the battery guns
　　By the gaunt and shadowy pine;
And his slow tread and still tread
　　Gives no warning sign.

The dark wave, the plumed wave,
　　It meets his eager glance;
And it sparkles 'neath the stars,
　　Like the glimmer of a lance—
A dark wave, a plumed wave,
　　On an emerald expanse.

A sharp clang, a steel clang,
　　And terror in the sound!
For the sentry, falcon-eyed,
　　In the camp ā spy hath found;
With a sharp clang, a steel clang,
　　The patriot is bound.

With calm brow, steady brow,
  He listens to his doom;
In his look there is no fear,
  Nor a shadow-trace of gloom;
But with calm brow and steady brow
  He robes him for the tomb.

In the long night, the still night,
  He kneels upon the sod;
And the brutal guards withhold
  E'en the solemn Word of God!
In the long night, the still night,
  He walks where Christ hath trod.

'Neath the blue morn, the sunny morn,
  He dies upon the tree;
And he mourns that he can lose
  But one life for Liberty;
And in the blue morn, the sunny morn,
  His spirit-wings are free.

But his last words, his message-words,
  They burn, lest friendly eye
Should read how proud and calm
  A patriot could die,
With his last words, his dying words,
  A soldier's battle-cry.

From the Fame-leaf and Angel-leaf,
  From monument and urn,
The sad of earth, the glad of heaven,
  His tragic fate shall learn ;
And on Fame-leaf and Angel-leaf
  The name of HALE shall burn.

                    FRANCIS MILES FINCH.

4

BATTLE OF TRENTON.

Dec. 26,
1776.

*This is an anonymous contemporary poem on the cross-
ing of the Delaware amid the ice, and the capture
of the Hessian Troops in Trenton.*

ON Christmas-day in seventy-six,
 Our ragged troops with bayonets fixed,
  For Trenton marched away.
The Delaware see! the boats below!
The light obscured by hail and snow!
  But no signs of dismay.

Our object was the Hessian band,
That dared invade fair freedom's land,
  And quarter in that place.
Great Washington he led us on,
Whose streaming flag, in storm or sun,
  Had never known disgrace.

In silent march we passed the night,
Each soldier panting for the fight,
    Though quite benumbed with frost.
Greene, on the left, at six began,
The right was led by Sullivan,
    Who ne'er a moment lost.

The pickets stormed, the alarm was spread,
The rebels risen from the dead
    Were marching into town.
Some scampered here, some scampered there,
And some for action did prepare;
    But soon their arms laid down.

Twelve hundred servile miscreants,
With all their colors, guns, and tents,
    Were trophies of the day.
The frolic o'er, the bright canteen
In centre, front, and rear was seen
    Driving fatigue away.

Now, brothers of the patriot bands,
Let 's sing deliverance from the hands
    Of arbitrary sway.
And as our life is but a span,
Let 's touch the tankard while we can,
    In memory of that day.

THE LITTLE BLACK-EYED REBEL.

Between
Sept. 26, 1777,
and
June 17, 1778.

The heroine's name was Mary Redmond, and she lived in Philadelphia. During the occupation of that town by the British, she was ever ready to aid in the secret delivery of the letters written home by the husbands and fathers fighting in the Continental Army. The poem is taken from "Young Folks' Centennial Rhymes" (Harpers, 1876).

A BOY drove into the city, his wagon loaded down
   With food to feed the people of the British-
      governed town;
And the little black-eyed rebel, so innocent and sly,
Was watching for his coming from the corner of her eye.

His face looked broad and honest, his hands were
      brown and tough,
The clothes he wore upon him were homespun, coarse,
      and rough;
But one there was who watched him, who long time
      lingered nigh,
And cast at him sweet glances from the corner of her eye.

53

He drove up to the market, he waited in the line;
His apples and potatoes were fresh and fair and fine;
But long and long he waited, and no one came to buy,
Save the black-eyed rebel, watching from the corner
    of her eye.

"Now who will buy my apples?" he shouted, long and
    loud;
And "Who wants my potatoes?" he repeated to the
    crowd;
But from all the people round him came no word of a
    reply,
Save the black-eyed rebel, answering from the corner
    of her eye.

For she knew that 'neath the lining of the coat he
    wore that day,
Were long letters from the husbands and the fathers far
    away,
Who were fighting for the freedom that they meant to
    gain or die;
And a tear like silver glistened in the corner of her eye.

But the treasures — how to get them? crept the question
     through her mind,
Since keen enemies were watching for what prizes they
     might find:
And she paused a while and pondered, with a pretty
     little sigh;
Then resolve crept through her features, and a shrewd-
     ness fired her eye.

So she resolutely walked up to the wagon old and red;
"May I have a dozen apples for a kiss?" she sweetly
     said:
And the brown face flushed to scarlet; for the boy was
     somewhat shy,
And he saw her laughing at him from the corner of
     her eye.

"You may have them all for nothing, and more, if you
     want," quoth he.
"I will have them, my good fellow, but can pay for
     them," said she;

And she clambered on the wagon, minding not who
    all were by,
With a laugh of reckless romping in the corner of her
    eye.

Clinging round his brawny neck, she clasped her fingers
    white and small,
And then whispered, " Quick ! the letters ! thrust them
    underneath my shawl !
Carry back again *this* package, and be sure that you
    are spry ! "
And she sweetly smiled upon him from the corner of
    her eye.

Loud the motley crowd were laughing at the strange,
    ungirlish freak,
And the boy was scared and panting, and so dashed
    he could not speak ;
And, " Miss, *I* have good apples," a bolder lad did cry ;
But she answered, " No, I thank you," from the corner
    of her eye.

With the news of loved ones absent to the dear friends
   they would greet,
Searching them who hungered for them, swift she glided
   through the street.
"There is nothing worth the doing that it does not
   pay to try,"
Thought the little black-eyed rebel, with a twinkle in
   her eye.

WILL CARLETON.

MOLLY MAGUIRE AT MONMOUTH.

June 28, 1778. *The battle of Monmouth was indecisive, but the Americans held the field, and the British retreated and remained inactive for the rest of the summer.*

ON the bloody field of Monmouth
    Flashed the guns of Greene and Wayne,
Fiercely roared the tide of battle,
    Thick the sward was heaped with slain.
Foremost, facing death and danger,
    Hessian, horse, and grenadier,
In the vanguard, fiercely fighting,
    Stood an Irish Cannonier.

Loudly roared his iron cannon,
    Mingling ever in the strife,
And beside him, firm and daring,
    Stood his faithful Irish wife.
Of her bold contempt of danger
    Greene and Lee's Brigades could tell,

Every one knew " Captain Molly,"
   And the army loved her well.

Surged the roar of battle round them,
   Swiftly flew the iron hail,
Forward dashed a thousand bayonets,
   That lone battery to assail.
From the foeman's foremost columns
   Swept a furious fusillade,
Mowing down the massed battalions
   In the ranks of Greene's Brigade.

Fast and faster worked the gunner,
   Soiled with powder, blood, and dust,
English bayonets shone before him,
   Shot and shell around him burst;
Still he fought with reckless daring,
   Stood and manned her long and well,
Till at last the gallant fellow
   Dead—beside his cannon fell.

With a bitter cry of sorrow,
　And a dark and angry frown,
Looked that band of gallant patriots
　At their gunner stricken down.
" Fall back, comrades, it is folly
　Thus to strive against the foe."
" No! not so," cried Irish Molly;
　" We can strike another blow."

*　*　*　*　*　*　*

Quickly leaped she to the cannon,
　In her fallen husband's place,
Sponged and rammed it fast and steady,
　Fired it in the foeman's face.
Flashed another ringing volley,
　Roared another from the gun;
" Boys, hurrah !" cried gallant Molly,
　" For the flag of Washington."

Greene's Brigade, though shorn and shattered,
　Slain and bleeding half their men,

When they heard that Irish slogan,
  Turned and charged the foe again.
Knox and Wayne and Morgan rally,
  To the front they forward wheel,
And before their rushing onset
  Clinton's English columns reel.

Still the cannon's voice in anger
  Rolled and rattled o'er the plain,
Till there lay in swarms around it
  Mangled heaps of Hessian slain.
" Forward! charge them with the bayonet!"
  'Twas the voice of Washington,
And there burst a fiery greeting
  From the Irish woman's gun.

Monckton falls; against his columns
  Leap the troops of Wayne and Lee,
And before their reeking bayonets
  Clinton's red battalions flee.
Morgan's rifles, fiercely flashing,
  Thin the foe's retreating ranks,

And behind them onward dashing
Ogden hovers on their flanks.

Fast they fly, these boasting Britons,
Who in all their glory came,
With their brutal Hessian hirelings
To wipe out our country's name.
Proudly floats the starry banner,
Monmouth's glorious field is won,
And in triumph Irish Molly
Stands beside her smoking gun.

WILLIAM COLLINS.

SONG OF MARION'S MEN.

1780–
1781.

*While the British Army held South Carolina, Marion
and Sumter gathered bands of partisans and waged
a vigorous guerilla warfare most harassing and de-
structive to the invader.*

OUR band is few, but true and tried,
　　Our leader frank and bold;
The British soldier trembles
　　When Marion's name is told.
Our fortress is the good greenwood
　　Our tent the cypress-tree;
We know the forest round us,
　　As seamen know the sea.
We know its walls of thorny vines,
　　Its glades of reedy grass,
Its safe and silent islands
　　Within the dark morass.

Wo to the English soldiery,
　　That little dread us near!

On them shall light at midnight
  A strange and sudden fear:
When, waking to their tents on fire
  They grasp their arms in vain,
And they who stand to face us
  Are beat to earth again.
And they who fly in terror deem
  A mighty host behind,
And hear the tramp of thousands
  Upon the hollow wind.

Then sweet the hour that brings release
  From danger and from toil;
We talk the battle over,
  And share the battle's spoil.
The woodland rings with laugh and shout,
  As if a hunt were up,
And woodland flowers are gathered
  To crown the soldier's cup.
With merry songs we mock the wind
  That in the pine-top grieves,

And slumber long and sweetly
  On beds of oaken leaves.

Well knows the fair and friendly moon
  The band that Marion leads—
The glitter of their rifles,
  The scampering of their steeds.
'Tis life to guide the fiery barb
  Across the moonlight plain;
'Tis life to feel the night-wind
  That lifts his tossing mane.
A moment in the British camp—
  A moment—and away
Back to the pathless forest,
  Before the peep of day.

Grave men there are by broad Santee,
  Grave men with hoary hairs;
Their hearts are all with Marion,
  For Marion are their prayers.
And lovely ladies greet our band
  With kindliest welcoming,

5

With smiles like those of summer,
 And tears like those of spring.
For them we wear these trusty arms,
 And lay them down no more
Till we have driven the Briton,
 For ever, from our shore.

WILLIAM CULLEN BRYANT.

THE BATTLE OF THE COWPENS.

Jan. 17,
1781.

*In 1781, most of the fighting was in the South, and the
first battle of importance was this, in which Morgan
defeated Tarleton. This poem is taken from "American Ballads" (Harpers, 1879).*

TO the Cowpens riding proudly, boasting loudly,
      rebels scorning,
Tarleton hurried, hot and eager for the fight;
From the Cowpens, sore confounded, on that January
      morning,
Tarleton hurried somewhat faster, fain to save him-
      self by flight.

In the morn he scorned us rarely, but he fairly found
      his error,
When his force was made our ready blows to feel;
When his horsemen and his footmen fled in wild and
      pallid terror
At the leaping of our bullets and the sweeping of
      our steel.

All the day before we fled them, and we led them to
    pursue us,
  Then at night on Thickety Mountain made our
    camp;
There we lay upon our rifles, slumber quickly coming
    to us,
  Spite the crackling of our camp-fires and our sen-
    tries' heavy tramp.

Morning on the mountain border ranged in order found
    our forces,
  Ere our scouts announced the coming of the foe;
While the hoar-frost lying near us, and the distant
    water-courses,
  Gleamed like silver in the sunlight, seemed like silver
    in their glow.

Morgan ranged us there to meet them, and to greet
    them with such favor
  That they scarce would care to follow us again;

In the rear, the Continentals—none were readier nor
      braver ;
  In the van, with ready rifles, steady, stern, our mount-
      ain men.

Washington, our trooper peerless, gay and fearless, with
      his forces
  Waiting panther-like upon the foe to fall,
Formed upon the slope behind us, where, on raw-boned
      country horses,
  Sat the sudden-summoned levies brought from Georgia
      - by M'Call.

Soon we heard a distant drumming, nearer coming, slow
      advancing—
  It was then upon the very nick of nine.
Soon upon the road from Spartanburg we saw their
      bayonets glancing,
  And the morning sunlight playing on their swaying
      scarlet line.

In the distance seen so dimly, they looked grimly;
    coming nearer,
  There was naught about them fearful, after all,
Until some one near me spoke in voice than falling
    water clearer,
  "Tarleton's quarter is the sword-blade, Tarleton's
    mercy is the ball."

Then the memory came unto me, heavy, gloomy, of my
    brother
  Who was slain while asking quarter at their hand;
Of that morning when was driven forth my sister and
    my mother
  From our cabin in the valley by the spoilers of the land.

I remembered of my brother slain, my mother spurned
    and beaten,
  Of my sister in her beauty brought to shame;
Of the wretches' jeers and laughter, as from mud-sill up
    to rafter
  Of the stripped and plundered cabin leapt the fierce,
    consuming flame.

But that memory had no power there in that hour
       there to depress me —
  No ! it stirred within my spirit fiercer ire ;
And I gripped my sword-hilt firmer, and my arm and
       heart grew stronger ;
  And I longed to meet the wronger on the sea of
       steel and fire.

On they came, our might disdaining, where the raining
       bullets leaden
  Pattered fast from scattered rifles on each wing ;
Here and there went down a foeman, and the ground
       began to redden ;
  And they drew them back a moment, like the tiger
       ere his spring.

Then said Morgan, " Ball and powder kill much prouder
       men than George's ;
  On your rifles and a careful aim rely.
They were trained in many battles — we in workshops,
       fields, and forges ;
  But we have our homes to fight for, and we do not
       fear to die."

Though our leader's words we cheered not, yet we
  feared not; we awaited,
 Strong of heart, the threatened onset, and it came:
Up the sloping hill-side swiftly rushed the foe so fiercely
  hated;
 On they came with gleaming bayonet 'mid the cannon's smoke and flame.

At their head rode Tarleton proudly; ringing loudly
  o'er the yelling
 Of his men we heard his voice's brazen tone;
With his dark eyes flashing fiercely, and his sombre
  features telling
 In their look the pride that filled him as the cham-
  pion of the throne.

On they pressed, when sudden flashing, ringing, crashing, came the firing
 Of our forward line upon their close-set ranks;
Then at coming of their steel, which moved with
  steadiness untiring,
 Fled our mountaineers, re-forming in good order on
  our flanks.

Then the combat's ranging anger, din, and clangor,
    round and o'er us
  Filled the forest, stirred the air, and shook the
    ground;
Charged with thunder-tramp the horsemen, while their
    sabres shone before us,
  Gleaming lightly, streaming brightly, through the
    smoky cloud around.

Through the pines and oaks resounding, madly bound-
    ing from the mountain,
  Leapt the rattle of the battle and the roar;
Fierce the hand-to-hand engaging, and the human
    freshet raging
  Of the surging current urging past a dark and bloody
    shore.

Soon the course of fight was altered; soon they faltered
    at the leaden
  Storm that smote them, and we saw their centre
    swerve.

Tarleton's eye flashed fierce in anger; Tarleton's face
    began to redden;
  Tarleton gave the closing order—"Bring to action
    the reserve!"

Up the slope his legion thundered, full three hundred;
    fiercely spurring,
  Cheering lustily, they fell upon our flanks;
And their worn and wearied comrades, at the sound so
    spirit-stirring,
  Felt a thrill of hope and courage pass along their
    shattered ranks.

By the wind the smoke-cloud lifted lightly drifted to
    the nor'ward,
  And displayed in all their pride the scarlet foe;
We beheld them, with a steady tramp and fearless,
    moving forward,
  With their banners proudly waving, and their bayonets
    levelled low.

Morgan gave his order clearly—" Fall back nearly to
  the border
Of the hill, and let the enemy come nigher ! "
Oh ! they thought we had retreated, and they charged
  in fierce disorder,
When out rang the voice of Howard—"To the right
  about, face !—Fire ! "

Then upon our very wheeling came the pealing of our
  volley,
And our balls made red a pathway down the hill ;
Broke the foe and shrank and cowered ; rang again
  the voice of Howard—
" Give the hireling dogs the bayonet ! "—and we did
  it with a will.

In the meanwhile one red-coated troop, unnoted, riding
  faster
Than their comrades on our rear in fury bore ;

But the light-horse led by Washington soon brought it
      to disaster,
  For they shattered it and scattered it, and smote it
      fast and sore.

Like a herd of startled cattle from the battle-field we
      drove them;
  In disorder down the Mill-gap road they fled;
Tarleton led them in the racing, fast he fled before our
      chasing,
  And he stopped not for the dying, and he stayed not
      for the dead.

Down the Mill-gap road they scurried and they hurried
      with such fleetness—
  We had never seen such running in our lives!
Ran they swifter than if seeking homes to taste do-
      mestic sweetness,
  Having many years been parted from their children
      and their wives.

Ah! for some no wife to meet them, child to greet
    them, friend to shield them!
To their home o'er ocean never sailing back;
After them the red avengers, bitter hate for death had
    sealed them,
    Yelped the dark and red-eyed sleuth-hound unrelent-
    ing on their track.

In their midst I saw one trooper, and around his waist
    I noted
Tied a simple silken scarf of blue and white;
When my vision grasped it clearly to my hatred I de-
    voted
    Him, from all the hireling wretches who were min-
    gled there in flight.

For that token in the summer had been from our cabin
    taken
By the robber-hands of wrongers of my kin;
'T was my sister's—for the moment things around me
    were forsaken;
    I was blind to fleeing foemen, I was deaf to battle's din.

Olden comrades round me lying dead or dying were
    unheeded;
  Vain to me they looked for succor in their need.
O'er the corses of the soldiers, through the gory pools
    I speeded,
  Driving rowel-deep my spurs within my madly bound-
    ing steed.

As I came he turned, and staring at my glaring eyes
    he shivered;
  Pallid fear went quickly o'er his features grim;
As he grasped his sword in terror, every nerve within
    him quivered,
  For his guilty spirit told him why I solely sought for
    him.

Though the stroke I dealt he parried, onward carried,
    down I bore him—
  Horse and rider—down together went the twain:
"Quarter!"—He! that scarf had doomed him! stood
    a son and brother o'er him;

Down through plume and brass and leather went my
sabre to the brain —
Ha! no music like that crushing through the skull-bone
to the brain.

THOMAS DUNN ENGLISH.

TO THE MEMORY OF THE AMERICANS WHO FELL AT EUTAW.

Sept. 8,
1781.

The fight at Eutaw Springs, although called a drawn battle, resulted in the withdrawal of the British troops from South Carolina.

A T Eutaw Springs the valiant died:
    Their limbs with dust are covered o'er—
Weep on, ye springs, your tearful tide;
    How many heroes are no more!

If, in this wreck of ruin, they
    Can yet be thought to claim the tear,
Oh, smite your gentle breast, and say,
    The friends of freedom slumber here!

Thou, who shalt trace this bloody plain,
    If goodness rules thy generous breast,
Sigh for the wasted rural reign;
    Sigh for the shepherds, sunk to rest!

Stranger, their humble graves adorn;
  You too may fall, and ask a tear;
'Tis not the beauty of the morn
  That proves the evening shall be clear,—

They saw their injur'd country's woe;
  The flaming town, the wasted field;
Then rush'd to meet the insulting foe;
  They took the spear—but left the shield.

Led by thy conquering genius, Greene,
  The Britons they compell'd to fly:
None distant view'd the fatal plain,
  None griev'd, in such a cause, to die,—

But, like the Parthians, fam'd of old,
  Who, flying, still their arrows threw;
These routed Britons, full as bold
  Retreated, and retreating slew.
6

Now rest in peace, our patriot band;
  Though far from Nature's limits thrown,
We trust they find a happier land,
  A brighter sunshine of their own.

PHILIP FRENEAU.

PERRY'S VICTORY ON LAKE ERIE.

Sept. 10, 1813.

Throughout the war of 1812 with Great Britain, the navy was more successful than the army. In the battle on Lake Erie, Commodore Oliver Hazard Perry captured six British vessels.

BRIGHT was the morn,—the waveless bay
   Shone like a mirror to the sun;
'Mid greenwood shades and meadows gay,
The matin birds their lays begun:
While swelling o'er the gloomy wood
Was heard the faintly-echoed roar,—
The dashing of the foaming flood,
That beat on Erie's distant shore.

The tawny wanderer of the wild
Paddled his painted birch canoe,
And, where the wave serenely smiled,
Swift as the darting falcon, flew;
He rowed along that peaceful bay,
And glanced its polished surface o'er,

Listening the billow far away,
That rolled on Erie's lonely shore.

What sounds awake my slumbering ear?
What echoes o'er the waters come?
It is the morning gun I hear,
The rolling of the distant drum.
Far o'er the bright illumined wave
I mark the flash,—I hear the roar,
That calls from sleep the slumbering brave,
To fight on Erie's lonely shore.

See how the starry banner floats,
And sparkles in the morning ray:
While sweetly swell the fife's gay notes
In echoes o'er the gleaming bay:
Flash follows flash, as through yon fleet
Columbia's cannons loudly roar,
And valiant tars the battle greet,
That storms on Erie's echoing shore.

O, who can tell what deeds were done,
When Britain's cross, on yonder wave,
Sunk 'neath Columbia's dazzling sun,
And met in Erie's flood its grave?
Who tell the triumphs of that day,
When, smiling at the cannon's roar,
Our hero, 'mid the bloody fray,
Conquered on Erie's echoing shore.

Though many a wounded bosom bleeds
For sire, for son, for lover dear,
Yet Sorrow smiles amid her weeds,—
Affliction dries her tender tear;
Oh! she exclaims, with glowing pride,
With ardent thoughts that wildly soar,
My sire, my son, my lover died,
Conquering on Erie's bloody shore.

Long shall my country bless that day,
When soared our Eagle to the skies;

Long, long in triumph's bright array,
That victory shall proudly rise :
And when our country's lights are gone,
And all its proudest days are o'er,
How will her fading courage dawn,
To think on Erie's bloody shore!

JAMES GATES PERCIVAL.

THE STAR SPANGLED BANNER.

Sept. 14, 1813.

After the British had brutally burned the Capitol at Washington, in August, 1813, they retired to their ships, and on September 12th and 13th, they made an attack on Baltimore. This poem was written on the morning after the Bombardment of Fort McHenry, while the author was a prisoner on the British fleet.

OH! say can you see, by the dawn's early light,
    What so proudly we hailed at the twilight's last
        gleaming;
Whose broad stripes and bright stars through the
        perilous fight,
    O'er the ramparts we watched, were so gallantly
        streaming?
And the rocket's red glare, the bombs bursting in air,
Gave proof through the night that our flag was still
        there;
    Oh, say, does that star-spangled banner yet wave
    O'er the land of the free and the home of the brave?

On the shore, dimly seen through the mists of the
      deep,
  Where the foe's haughty host in dread silence
      reposes,
What is that which the breeze o'er the towering steep
  As it fitfully blows, half conceals, half discloses?
Now it catches the gleam of the morning's first beam;
Its full glory reflected now shines on the stream;
  'T is the star-spangled banner! Oh! long may it
      wave
  O'er the land of the free and home of the brave!

And where is the band who so vauntingly swore,
  Mid the havoc of war and the battle's confusion,
A home and a country they 'd leave us no more?
  Their blood hath washed out their foul footsteps'
      pollution;
No refuge could save the hireling and slave
From the terror of flight, or the gloom of the grave,
  And the star-spangled banner in triumph doth wave
  O'er the land of the free and the home of the brave!

Oh! thus be it ever, when freemen shall stand

    Between their loved home and the war's desolation;

Blessed with victory and peace, may the Heaven-rescued

      land

    Praise the Power that hath made and preserved us a

      nation.

Then conquer we must, for our cause it is just,

And this be our motto, "In God is our trust":

    And the star-spangled banner in triumph shall wave

    O'er the land of the free and the home of the brave.

FRANCIS SCOTT KEY.

THE BATTLE OF NEW ORLEANS.

Jan. 8,
1815,

*The treaty of peace between Great Britain and the
United States was signed at Ghent, December 14,
1814; but before the news crossed the ocean, Pakenham, with twelve thousand British veterans, at-
tacked New Orleans defended by Andrew Jackson
with five thousand Americans, mostly militia. The
British were repulsed with a loss of two thousand;
the American loss was trifling.*

HERE, in my rude log cabin,
  Few poorer men there be
Among the mountain ranges
  Of Eastern Tennessee.
My limbs are weak and shrunken,
  White hairs upon my brow,
My dog—lie still, old fellow!—
  My sole companion now.
Yet I, when young and lusty,
  Have gone through stirring scenes,
For I went down with Carroll
  To fight at New Orleans.

90

You say you'd like to hear me
　The stirring story tell
Of those who stood the battle
　And those who fighting fell.
Short work to count our losses—
　We stood and dropp'd the foe
As easily as by firelight
　Men shoot the buck or doe.
And while they fell by hundreds
　Upon the bloody plain,
Of us, fourteen were wounded,
　And only eight were slain.

The eighth of January,
　Before the break of day,
Our raw and hasty levies
　Were brought into array.
No cotton-bales before us—
　Some fool that falsehood told;
Before us was an earthwork,
　Built from the swampy mold.

And there we stood in silence,
And waited with a frown,
To greet with bloody welcome
The bull-dogs of the Crown.

The heavy fog of morning
Still hid the plain from sight,
When came a thread of scarlet
Marked faintly in the white.
We fired a single cannon,
And as its thunders roll'd
The mist before us lifted
In many a heavy fold.
The mist before us lifted,
And in their bravery fine
Came rushing to their ruin
The fearless British line.

Then from our waiting cannons
Leap'd forth the deadly flame,
To meet the advancing columns
That swift and steady came.

The thirty-twos of Crowley
  And Bluchi's twenty-four,
To Spotts's eighteen-pounders
  Responded with their roar,
Sending the grape-shot deadly
  That marked its pathway plain,
And paved the road it travell'd
  With corpses of the slain.

Our rifles firmly grasping,
  And heedless of the din,
We stood in silence waiting
  For orders to begin.
Our fingers on the triggers,
  Our hearts, with anger stirr'd,
Grew still more fierce and eager
  As Jackson's voice was heard:
"Stand steady! Waste no powder
  Wait till your shots will tell!
To-day the work you finish —
  See that you do it well!"

Their columns drawing nearer,
  We felt our patience tire,
When came the voice of Carroll,
  Distinct and measured, " Fire ! "
Oh ! then you should have mark'd us
  Our volleys on them pour—
Have heard our joyous rifles
  Ring sharply through the roar,
And seen their foremost columns
  Melt hastily away
As snow in mountain gorges
  Before the floods of May.

They soon reform'd their columns,
  And 'mid the fatal rain
We never ceased to hurtle
  Came to their work again.
The Forty-fourth is with them,
  That first its laurels won
With stout old Abercrombie
  Beneath an eastern sun.

It rushes to the battle,
  And, though within the rear
Its leader is a laggard,
  It shows no signs of fear.

It did not need its colonel,
  For soon there came. instead
An eagle-eyed commander,
  And on its march he led.
'Twas Pakenham, in person,
  The leader of the field ;
I knew it by the cheering
  That loudly round him peal'd ;
And by his quick, sharp movement,
  We felt his heart was stirr'd,
As when at Salamanca,
  He led the fighting Third.

I raised my rifle quickly,
  I sighted at his breast,
God save the gallant leader
  And take him to his rest !

I did not draw the trigger,
I could not for my life.
So calm he sat his charger
Amid the deadly strife,
That in my fiercest moment
A prayer arose from me,—
God save that gallant leader,
Our foeman though he be.

Sir Edward's charger staggers:
He leaps at once to ground,
And ere the beast falls bleeding
Another horse is found.
His right arm falls—'tis wounded;
He waves on high his left;
In vain he leads the movement,
The ranks in twain are cleft.
The men in scarlet waver
Before the men in brown,
And fly in utter panic—
The soldiers of the Crown!

I thought the work was over,
　But nearer shouts were heard,
And came, with Gibbs to head it,
　The gallant Ninety-third.
Then Pakenham, exulting,
　With proud and joyous glance,
Cried, " Children of the tartan—
　Bold Highlanders—advance!
Advance to scale the breast-works
　And drive them from their hold,
And show the stanchless courage
　That mark'd your sires of old!"

His voice as yet was ringing,
　When, quick as light, there came
The roaring of a cannon,
　And earth seemed all aflame.
Who causes thus the thunder
　The doom of men to speak?
It is the Baritarian,
　The fearless Dominique.

Down through the marshall'd Scotsmen
　The step of death is heard,
And by the fierce tornado
　Falls half the Ninety-third.

The smoke passed slowly upward,
　And, as it soared on high,
I saw the brave commander
　In dying anguish lie.
They bear him from the battle
　Who never fled the foe;
Unmoved by death around them
　His bearers softly go.
In vain their care, so gentle,
　Fades earth and all its scenes;
The man of Salamanca
　Lies dead at New Orleans.

But where were his lieutenants?
　Had they in terror fled?
No! Keane was sorely wounded
　And Gibbs as good as dead.

Brave Wilkinson commanding,
  A major of brigade,
The shatter'd force to rally,
  A final effort made.
He led it up our ramparts,
  Small glory did he gain—
Our captives some, while othe 's fled,
  And he himself was slain.

The stormers had retreated,
  The bloody work was o'er ;
The feet of the invaders
  Were seen to leave our shore.
We rested on our rifles
  And talk'd about the fight,
When came a sudden murmur
  Like fire from left to right ;
We turned and saw our chieftain,
  And then, good friend of mine,
You should have heard the cheering
  That rang along the line.

For well our men remembered
　How little when they came,
Had they but native courage,
　And trust in Jackson's name;
How through the day he labored,
　How kept the vigils still,
Till discipline controlled us,
　A stronger power than will;
And how he hurled us at them
　Within the evening hour,
That red night in December,
　And made us feel our power.

In answer to our shouting
　Fire lit his eye of gray;
Erect, but thin and pallid,
　He passed upon his bay.
Weak from the baffled fever,
　And shrunken in each limb,
The swamps of Alabama
　Had done their work on him.

But spite of that and lasting,
And hours of sleepless care,
The soul of Andrew Jackson
Shone forth in glory there.

THOMAS DUNN ENGLISH.

THE AMERICAN FLAG.

May 29,
1819.

*The penultimate quatrain [enclosed in brackets] ended
the poem as Drake wrote it, but Fitz Greene
Halleck suggested the final four lines, and Drake
accepted his friend's quatrain in place of his own.*

WHEN Freedom, from her mountain height,
  Unfurled her standard to the air,
She tore the azure robe of night,
  And set the stars of glory there!
She mingled with its gorgeous dyes
The milky baldric of the skies,
And striped its pure celestial white
With streakings of the morning light,
Then, from his mansion in the sun,
She called her eagle-bearer down,
And gave into his mighty hand
The symbol of her chosen land!

Majestic monarch of the cloud!
  Who rear'st aloft thy regal form,

To hear the tempest-tramping loud,
And see the lightning-lances driven,
   When stride the warriors of the storm,
And rolls the thunder-drum of heaven!
Child of the sun! to thee 'tis given
   To guard the banner of the free,
To hover in the sulphur smoke,
To ward away the battle stroke,
And bid its blendings shine afar,
Like rainbows on the cloud of war,
   The harbingers of victory!

Flag of the brave! thy folds shall fly,
The sign of hope and triumph high!
When speaks the signal-trumpet tone,
And the long line comes gleaming on,
(Ere yet the life-blood, warm and wet,
Has dimmed the glist'ning bayonet),
Each soldier's eye shall brightly turn
To where thy meteor-glories burn,
And, as his springing steps advance,
Catch war and vengeance from the glance!

And when the cannon-mouthings loud
Heave in wild wreaths the battle-shroud,
And gory sabres rise and fall,
Like shoots of flame on midnight's pall!
There shall thy victor-glances glow,
  And cowering foes shall shrink beneath,
Each gallant arm that strikes below,
  The lovely messenger of death.

Flag of the seas! on ocean's wave
Thy star shall glitter o'er the brave;
When Death, careering on the gale,
Sweeps darkly round the bellied sail,
And frighted waves rush wildly back
Before the broad-side's reeling rack,
The dying wanderer of the sea
Shall look, at once, to heaven and thee,
And smile, to see thy splendors fly,
In triumph, o'er his closing eye.

Flag of the free heart's hope and home,
  By angel hands to valor given!

Thy stars have lit the welkin dome,
  And all thy hues were born in heaven!
[And fixed as yonder orb divine,
  That saw thy bannered blaze unfurled,
Shall thy proud stars resplendent shine,
  The guard and glory of the world.]
Forever float that standard sheet!
  Where breathes the foe but falls before us?
With Freedom's soil beneath our feet,
  And Freedom's banner streaming o'er us!

JOSEPH RODMAN DRAKE.

OLD IRONSIDES.

Sept. 16,
1830.

The frigate Constitution was launched in 1797, and took part in the war with Tripoli in 1804. In 1812 she captured the British Guerrière on August 19th, and the British Java on December 29th. After the war she served as a training ship. In 1830 it was proposed to break her up, which called forth this indignant poem. In 1876 she was refitted, and in 1878 she took over the American exhibits to the Paris Exhibition. She now lies out of commission in Rotten Row, at the Brooklyn Navy Yard.

AY, tear her tattered ensign down!
 Long has it waved on high,
And many an eye has danced to see
 That banner in the sky;
Beneath it rung the battle shout,
 And burst the cannon's roar; —
The meteor of the ocean air
 Shall sweep the clouds no more!

Her deck, once red with heroes' blood,
 Where knelt the vanquished foe,

When winds were hurrying o'er the flood
　And waves were white below,
No more shall feel the victor's tread,
　Or know the conquered knee; —
The harpies of the shore shall pluck
　The eagle of the sea !

Oh, better that her shattered hulk
　Should sink beneath the wave;
Her thunders shook the mighty deep,
　And there should be her grave;
Nail to the mast her holy flag,
　Set every threadbare sail,
And give her to the God of storms, —
　The lightning and the gale !

OLIVER WENDELL HOLMES.

MONTEREY.

Sept. 19–24,
. 1846.

*The assaulting American army at the attack on Monterey
numbered six thousand six hundred and twenty-five;
the defeated Mexicans were about ten thousand.*

WE were not many — we who stood
　　Before the iron sleet that day;
Yet many a gallant spirit would
Give half his years if but he could
　　Have with us been at Monterey.

Now here, now there, the shot it hailed
　　In deadly drifts of fiery spray,
Yet not a single soldier quailed
When wounded comrades round them wailed
　　Their dying shout at Monterey.

And on — still on our column kept,
　　Through walls of flame, its withering way;
Where fell the dead, the living stept,
Still charging on the guns which swept
　　The slippery streets of Monterey.

The foe himself recoiled aghast,
  When, striking where he strongest lay,
We swooped his flanking batteries past,
And, braving full their murderous blast,
  Stormed home the towers of Monterey.

Our banners on those turrets wave,
  And there our evening bugles play;
Where orange-boughs above their grave
Keep green the memory of the brave
  Who fought and fell at Monterey.

We are not many — we who pressed
  Beside the brave who fell that day;
But who of us has not confessed
He 'd rather share their warrior rest
  Than not have been at Monterey?

                    CHARLES FENNO HOFFMAN.

THE BIVOUAC OF THE DEAD.

Feb. 22, 23,
1847.

*This poem was written to commemorate the bringing
home of the bodies of the Kentucky soldiers who fell
at Buena Vista, and their burial at Frankfort at the
cost of the State.*

THE muffled drum's sad roll has beat
  The soldier's last tattoo;
No more on life's parade shall meet
  That brave and fallen few.
On fame's eternal camping ground
  Their silent tents are spread,
And glory guards, with solemn round,
  The bivouac of the dead.

No rumor of the foe's advance
  Now swells upon the wind;
No troubled thought at midnight haunts
  Of loved ones left behind;
No vision of the morrow's strife
  The warrior's dream alarms;

No braying horn, nor screaming fife,
  At dawn shall call to arms.

Their shivered swords are red with rust,
  Their plumèd heads are bowed;
Their haughty banner, trailed in dust,
  Is now their martial shroud.
And plenteous funeral tears have washed
  The red stains from each brow,
And the proud forms, by battle gashed,
  Are free from anguish now.

The neighing troop, the flashing blade,
  The bugle's stirring blast,
The charge, the dreadful cannonade,
  The din and shout are past;
Nor war's wild note nor glory's peal
  Shall thrill with fierce delight
Those breasts that never more may feel
  The rapture of the fight.

Like the fierce northern hurricane
  That sweeps his great plateau,
Flushed with the triumph yet to gain,
  Came down the serried foe.
Who heard the thunder of the fray
  Break o'er the field beneath,
Knew well the watchword of that day
  Was " Victory or death."

Long had the doubtful conflict raged
  O'er all that stricken plain,
For never fiercer fight had waged
  The vengeful blood of Spain;
And still the storm of battle blew,
  Still swelled the gory tide;
Not long, our stout old chieftain knew,
  Such odds his strength could bide.

'T was in that hour his stern command
  Called to a martyr's grave
The flower of his belovèd land,
  The nation's flag to save.

By rivers of their father's gore
   His first-born laurels grew,
And well he deemed the sons would pour
   Their lives for glory too.

Full many a norther's breath has swept
   O'er Angostura's plain —
And long the pitying sky has wept
   Above the mouldering slain.
The raven's scream, or eagle's flight,
   Or shepherd's pensive lay,
Alone awakes each sullen height
   That frowned o'er that dread fray.

Sons of the Dark and Bloody Ground,
   Ye must not slumber there,
Where stranger steps and tongues resound
   Along the heedless air;
Your own proud land's heroic soil
   Shall be your fitter grave;
She claims from war his richest spoil —
   The ashes of her brave.
8

So, 'neath their parent turf they rest,
　　Far from the gory field,
Borne to a Spartan mother's breast,
　　On many a bloody shield;
The sunshine of their native sky
　　Smiles sadly on them here,
And kindred eyes and hearts watch by
　　The heroes' sepulchre.

Rest on, embalmed and sainted dead,
　　Dear as the blood ye gave;
No impious footstep here shall tread
　　The herbage of your grave;
Nor shall your glory be forgot
　　While Fame her record keeps,
Or Honor points the hallowed spot
　　Where Valor proudly sleeps.

Yon marble minstrel's voiceless stone,
　　In deathless song shall tell,
When many a vanished age hath flown,
　　The story how ye fell;

Nor wreck, nor change, nor winter's blight,
   Nor Time's remorseless doom,
Shall dim one ray of glory's light
   That gilds your deathless tomb.

THEODORE O'HARA.

HOW OLD BROWN TOOK HARPER'S FERRY.

Oct. 16–
Dec. 2,
1859.

It was on Sunday, October 16th, that John Brown took the Arsenal at Harper's Ferry. On the 18th he was captured. On December 2d he was hanged. One year later began the War which caused the abolition of slavery.

JOHN BROWN in Kansas settled, like a steadfast Yankee farmer,

Brave and godly, with four sons, all stalwart men of might.

There he spoke aloud for freedom, and the Border-strife grew warmer,

Till the Rangers fired his dwelling, in his absence, in the night;

And Old Brown,

Osawatomie Brown,

Came homeward in the morning — to find his house burned down.

116

Then he grasped his trusty rifle and boldly fought for
    freedom;
  Smote from border unto border the fierce, invading
    band;
And he and his brave boys vowed — so might Heaven
    help and speed 'em! —
  They would save those grand old prairies from the
    curse that blights the land;
          And Old Brown,
          Osawatomie Brown,
  Said, " Boys, the Lord will aid us!" and he shoved
    his ramrod down.

And the Lord *did* aid these men, and they labored day
    and even,
  Saving Kansas from its peril; and their very lives
    seemed charmed,
Till the ruffians killed one son, in the blessed light of
    Heaven, —
  In cold blood the fellows slew him, as he journeyed,
    all unarmed;

Then Old Brown,
Osawatomie Brown,
Shed not a tear, but shut his teeth, and frowned a
terrible frown!

Then they seized another brave boy, — not amid the
heat of battle,
But in peace, behind his ploughshare, — and they
loaded him with chains,
And with pikes, before their horses, even as they goad
their cattle,
Drove him cruelly, for their sport, and at last blew
out his brains;
Then Old Brown,
Osawatomie Brown,
Raised his right hand up to Heaven, calling Heaven's
vengeance down.

And he swore a fearful oath, by the name of the
Almighty,
He would hunt this ravening evil that had scathed
and torn him so;

He would seize it by the vitals; he would crush it day
  and night; he
 Would so pursue its footsteps, so return it blow for
  blow,
    That Old Brown,
    Osawatomie Brown,
Should be a name to swear by, in backwoods or in
  town!

Then his beard became more grizzled, and his wild
  blue eye grew wilder,
 And more sharply curved his hawk's-nose, snuffing
  battle from afar;
And he and the two boys left, though the Kansas
  strife waxed milder,
 Grew more sullen, till was over the bloody Border
  War,
    And Old Brown,
    Osawatomie Brown,
Had gone crazy, as they reckoned by his fearful glare
  and frown.

So he left the plains of Kansas and their bitter woes
    behind him.
Slipt off into Virginia, where the statesmen all are born,
Hired a farm by Harper's Ferry, and no one knew
    where to find him,
    Or whether he 'd turned parson, or was jacketed and
    shorn;
              For Old Brown,
              Osawatomie Brown,
Mad as he was, knew texts enough to wear a parson's
    gown

He bought no ploughs and harrows, spades and shovels,
    and such trifles;
    But quietly to his rancho there came, by every train,
Boxes full of pikes and pistols, and his well-beloved
    Sharp's rifles;
    And eighteen other madmen joined their leader there
    again.
              Says Old Brown,
              Osawatomie Brown,

" Boys, we 've got an army large enough to march and
    take the town!

" Take the town, and seize the muskets, free the negroes
    and then arm them;
  Carry the County and the State, ay, and all the potent
    South.
On their own heads be the slaughter, if their victims
    rise to harm them —
  These Virginians! who believed not, nor would heed
    the warning mouth."
                Says Old Brown,
                Osawatomie Brown,
" The world shall see a Republic, or my name is not
    John Brown."

'T was the sixteenth of October, on the evening of a
    Sunday:
  " This good work," declared the captain, "shall be
    on a holy night!"
It was on a Sunday evening, and before the noon of
    Monday,

With two sons, and Captain Stephens, fifteen pri-
vates — black and white,
> Captain Brown,
> Osawatomie Brown,
Marched across the bridged Potomac, and knocked the
sentry down;

Took the guarded armory-building, and the muskets and
the cannon;
Captured all the county majors and the colonels, one
by one;
Scared to death each gallant scion of Virginia they ran
on,
And before the noon of Monday, I say, the deed
was done.
> Mad Old Brown,
> Osawatomie Brown,
With his eighteen other crazy men, went in and took
the town.

Very little noise and bluster, little smell of powder
made he;   .

It was all done in the midnight, like the Emperor's
  coup d'état.
" Cut the wires! Stop the rail-cars! Hold the streets
    and bridges!" said he,
  Then declared the new Republic, with himself for
    guiding star, —
        This Old Brown,
        Osawatomie Brown;
And the bold two thousand citizens ran off and left the town.

Then was riding and railroading and expressing here
    and thither;
  And the Martinsburg Sharpshooters and the Charles-
    town Volunteers,
And the Shepherdstown and Winchester Militia hastened
    whither
  Old Brown was said to muster his ten thousand
    grenadiers.
        General Brown!
        Osawatomie Brown!!
Behind whose rampant banner all the North was pouring
    down.

But at last, 't is said, some prisoners escaped from Old
    Brown's durance,
  And the effervescent valor of the Chivalry broke
    out,
When they learned that nineteen madmen had the mar-
    velous assurance —
  Only nineteen — thus to seize the place and drive
    them straight about;
            And Old Brown,
           Osawatomie Brown,
Found an army come to take him, encamped around
    the town.

But to storm, with all the forces I have mentioned,
    was too risky;
  So they hurried off to Richmond for the Government
    Marines,
Tore them from their weeping matrons, fired their souls
    with Bourbon whiskey,
  Till they battered down Brown's castle with their
    ladders and machines;

And Old Brown,
Osawatomie Brown,
Received three bayonet stabs, and a cut on his brave
old crown.

Tallyho! the old Virginia gentry gather to the baying!
  In they rushed and killed the game, shooting lustily
    away;
And whene'er they slew a rebel, those who came too
    late for slaying,
  Not to lose a share of glory, fired their bullets in
    his clay;
And Old Brown,
Osawatomie Brown,
Saw his sons fall dead beside him, and between them
laid him down.

How the conquerors wore their laurels; how they
    hastened on the trial;
  How Old Brown was placed, half dying, on the
    Charlestown court-house floor;

How he spoke his grand oration, in the scorn of all denial;
What the brave old madman told them, — these are
known the country o'er.
"Hang Old Brown,
Osawatomie Brown,"
Said the judge, "and all such rebels!" with his most
judicial frown.

But, Virginians, don't do it! for I tell you that the
flagon,
Filled with blood of Old Brown's offspring, was first
poured by Southern hands;
And each drop from Old Brown's life-veins, like the
red gore of the dragon,
May spring up a vengeful Fury, hissing through your
slave-worn lands!
And Old Brown,
Osawatomie Brown,
May trouble you more than ever, when you 've nailed
his coffin down!

EDMUND CLARENCE STEDMAN.

APOCALYPSE.

April 19, 1861. *The first life lost in the battle with rebellion was that of Private Arthur Ladd, of the Sixth Massachusetts, killed in the attack of the Baltimore mob on his regiment.*

STRAIGHT to his heart the bullet crushed;
   Down from his breast the red blood gushed,
And o'er his face a glory rushed.

A sudden spasm shook his frame,
And in his ears there went and came
A sound as of devouring flame.

Which in a moment ceased, and then
The great light clasped his brows again,
So that they shone like Stephen's when

Saul stood apart a little space
And shook with shuddering awe to trace
God's splendors settling o'er his face.

Thus, like a king, erect in pride,
Raising clean hands toward heaven, he cried:
"All hail the Stars and Stripes!" and died.

Died grandly.   But before he fell —
(O blessedness ineffable!)
Vision apocalyptical

Was granted to him, and his eyes,
All radiant with glad surprise,
Looked forward through the Centuries,

And saw the seeds which sages cast
In the world's soil in cycles past,
Spring up and blossom at the last;

Saw how the souls of men had grown,
And where the scythes of Truth had mown
Clear space for Liberty's white throne;

Saw how, by sorrow tried and proved,
The blackening stains had been removed
Forever from the land he loved;

Saw Treason crushed and Freedom crowned,
And clamorous Faction, gagged and bound,
Gasping its life out on the ground.

* * * * *

With far-off vision gazing clear
Beyond this gloomy atmosphere
Which shuts us out with doubt and fear

He — marking how her high increase
Ran greatening in perpetual lease
Through balmy years of odorous Peace

Greeted in one transcendent cry
Of intense, passionate ecstacy
The sight which thrilled him utterly;

Saluting, with most proud disdain
Of murder and of mortal pain,
The vision which shall be again!

9

So, lifted with prophetic pride,
Raised conquering hands to heaven and cried:
" All hail the Stars and Stripes!" and died.

                                    RICHARD REALF.

SCOTT AND THE VETERAN.

May 13,
1861.

AN old and crippled veteran to the War Department
came ;
He sought the Chief who led him on many a field of
fame, —
The Chief who shouted " Forward ! " where'er his banner
rose,
And bore its stars in triumph behind the flying foes.

" Have you forgotten, General," the battered soldier
cried,
" The days of Eighteen Hundred Twelve, when I was
at your side ?
Have you forgotten Johnson, that fought at Lundy's
Lane ?
'T is true, I 'm old and pensioned, but I want to fight
again."

" Have I forgotten?" said the Chief; " my brave old
    soldier, No !
And here 's the hand I gave you then, and let it tell
    you so :
But you have done your share, my friend; you 're
    crippled, old, and gray,
And we have need of younger arms and fresher blood
    to-day."

" But, General," cried the veteran, a flush upon his
    brow,
" The very men who fought with us, they say, are
    traitors now ;
They 've torn the flag of Lundy's Lane, — our old red,
    white, and blue ;
And while a drop of blood is left, I 'll show that drop
    is true.

" I 'm not so weak but I can strike, and I 've a good
    old gun
To get the range of traitors' hearts, and pick them, one
    by one.

Your Minié rifles, and such arms, it a'n't worth while
    to try :
I could n't get the hang o' them, but I 'll keep my
    powder dry ! "

" God bless you, comrade ! " said the Chief; " God
    bless your loyal heart !
But younger men are in the field, and claim to have
    their part ;
They 'll plant our sacred banner in each rebellious
    town,
And woe, henceforth, to any hand that dares to pull it
    down ! "

" But, General," — still persisting, the weeping veteran
    cried,
" I 'm young enough to follow, so long as you 're my
    guide ;
And some, you know, must bite the dust, and that, at
    least, can I, —
So give the young ones place to fight, but me a place
    to die !

" If they should fire on Pickens, let the Colonel in
    command
Put me upon the rampart, with the flag-staff in my hand :
No odds how hot the cannon-smoke, or how the shell
    may fly ;
I 'll hold the Stars and Stripes aloft, and hold them till
    I die !

" I 'm ready, General, so you let a post to me be given,
Where Washington can see me, as he looks from highest
    heaven,
And say to Putnam at his side, or, may be, General
    Wayne :
' There stands old Billy Johnson, that fought at Lundy's
    Lane ! '

" And when the fight is hottest, before the traitors fly,
When shell and ball are screeching and bursting in the sky,
If any shot should hit me, and lay me on my face,
My soul would go to Washington's, and not to Arnold's
    place ! "

                              BAYARD TAYLOR.

THE PICKET GUARD.

Sept., 1861.

The stereotyped announcement, "All Quiet on the Potomac," was followed one day in September, 1861, by the words, "A Picket Shot," and these so moved the authoress that she wrote this poem on the impulse of the moment.

"ALL quiet along the Potomac," they say,
   "Except now and then a stray picket
Is shot, as he walks on his beat, to and fro,
   By a rifleman hid in the thicket.
'T is nothing — a private or two, now and then,
   Will not count in the news of the battle;
Not an officer lost — only one of the men,
   Moaning out, all alone, the death rattle."

All quiet along the Potomac to-night,
   Where the soldiers lie peacefully dreaming;
Their tents in the rays of the clear autumn moon,
   Or the light of the watch-fires, are gleaming.

A tremulous sigh, as the gentle night-wind
  Through the forest-leaves softly is creeping;
While stars up above, with their glittering eyes,
  Keep guard — for the army is sleeping.

There 's only the sound of the lone sentry's tread,
  As he tramps from the rock to the fountain,
And thinks of the two in the low trundle-bed
  Far away in the cot on the mountain.
His musket falls slack — his face, dark and grim,
  Grows gentle with memories tender,
As he mutters a prayer for the children asleep —
  For their mother — may Heaven defend her!

The moon seems to shine just as brightly as then,
  That night, when the love yet unspoken
Leaped up to his lips — when low-murmured vows
  Were pledged to be ever unbroken.
Then drawing his sleeve roughly over his eyes,
  He dashes off tears that are welling,

And gathers his gun closer up to its place
  As if to keep down the heart-swelling.

He passes the fountain, the blasted pine-tree —
  The footstep is lagging and weary;
Yet onward he goes, through the broad belt of light,
  Toward the shades of the forest so dreary.
Hark! was it the night-wind that rustled the leaves?
  Was it moonlight so wondrously flashing?
It looked like a rifle — "Ah! Mary, good-bye!"
  And the life-blood is ebbing and plashing.

All quiet along the Potomac to-night,
  No sound save the rush of the river;
While soft falls the dew on the face of the dead —
  The picket's off duty forever.

Ethel Lynn Beers.

THE WASHERS OF THE SHROUD.

Oct.,
1861.

ALONG a river-side, I know not where,
    I walked one night in mystery of dream;
A chill creeps curdling yet beneath my hair,
To think what chanced me by the pallid gleam
Of a moon-wraith that waned through haunted air.

Pale fireflies pulsed within the meadow-mist
Their halos, wavering thistledowns of light;
The loon, that seemed to mock some goblin tryst,
Laughed; and the echoes, huddling in affright,
Like Odin's hounds, fled baying down the night.

Then all was silent, till there smote my ear
A movement in the stream that checked my breath:
Was it the slow plash of a wading deer?
But something said, "This water is of Death!
The Sisters wash a shroud,— ill thing to hear!"

I, looking then, beheld the ancient Three
Known to the Greek's and to the Northman's creed,
That sit in shadow of the mystic Tree,
Still crooning, as they weave their endless brede,
One song: "Time was, Time is, and Time shall be."

No wrinkled crones were they, as I had deemed,
But fair as yesterday, to-day, to-morrow,
To mourner, lover, poet, ever seemed;
Something too high for joy, too deep for sorrow,
Thrilled in their tones, and from their faces gleamed.

"Still men and nations reap as they have strawn,"
So sang they, working at their task the while;
"The fatal raiment must be cleansed ere dawn;
For Austria? Italy? the Sea-Queen's isle?
O'er what quenched grandeur must our shroud be
    drawn?

"Or is it for a younger, fairer corse,
That gathered States for children round his knees,
That tamed the wave to be his posting-horse,

Feller of forests, linker of the seas,
Bridge-builder, hammerer, youngest son of Thor's?

" What make we, murmur'st thou? and what are we?
When empires must be wound, we bring the shroud,
The time-old web of the implacable Three:
Is it too coarse for him, the young and proud?
Earth's mightiest deigned to wear it, — why not he?"

" Is there no hope?" I moaned, "so strong, so fair!
Our Fowler whose proud bird would brook erewhile
No rival's swoop in all our western air!
Gather the ravens, then, in funeral file
For him, life's morn yet golden in his hair?

" Leave me not hopeless, ye unpitying dames!
I see, half seeing. Tell me, ye who scanned
The stars, Earth's elders, still must noblest aims
Be traced upon oblivious ocean-sands?
Must Hesper join the wailing ghosts of names?"

" When grass-blades stiffen with red battle-dew,
Ye deem we choose the victor and the slain:

Say, choose we them that shall be leal and true
To the heart's longing, the high faith of brain ?
Yet there the victory lies, if ye but knew.

" Three roots bear up Dominion : Knowledge, Will, —
These twain are strong, but stronger yet the third, —
Obedience, — 't is the great tap-root that still,
Knit round the rock of Duty, is not stirred,
Though Heaven-loosed tempests spend their utmost
      skill.

" Is the doom sealed for Hesper ? 'T is not we
Denounce it, but the Law before all time :
The brave makes danger opportunity ;
The waverer, paltering with the chance sublime,
Dwarfs it to peril : which shall Hesper be ?

" Hath he let vultures climb his eagle's seat
To make Jove's bolts purveyors of their maw ?
Hath he the Many's plaudits found more sweet
Than Wisdom ? held Opinion's wind for Law ?
Then let him hearken for the doomster's feet !

"Rough are the steps, slow-hewn in flintiest rock,
States climb to power by; slippery those with gold
Down which they stumble to eternal mock:
No chafferer's hand shall long the sceptre hold,
Who, given a Fate to shape, would sell the block.

"We sing old Sagas, songs of weal and woe,
Mystic because too cheaply understood;
Dark sayings are not ours; men hear and know,
See Evil weak, see strength alone in Good,
Yet hope to stem God's fire with walls of tow.

"Time Was unlocks the riddle of Time Is,
That offers choice of glory or of gloom;
The solver makes Time Shall Be surely his.
But hasten, Sisters! for even now the tomb
Grates its slow hinge and calls from the abyss."

"But not for him," I cried, "not yet for him,
Whose large horizon, westering, star by star
Wins from the void to where on Ocean's rim

The sunset shuts the world with golden bar,
Not yet his thews shall fail, his eye grow dim!

" His shall be larger manhood, saved for those
That walk unblenching through the trial-fires;
Not suffering, but faint heart, is worst of woes,
And he no base-born son of craven sires,
Whose eye need blench confronted with his foes.

" Tears may be ours, but proud, for those who win
Death's royal purple in the foeman's lines;
Peace, too, brings tears; and 'mid the battle-din,
The wiser ear some text of God divines,
For the sheathed blade may rust with darker sin.

" God, give us peace! not such as lulls to sleep,
But sword on thigh, and brow with purpose knit!
And let our Ship of State to harbor sweep,
Her ports all up, her battle-lanterns lit,
And her leashed thunders gathering for their leap!"

So cried I with clenched hands and passionate pain,
Thinking of dear ones by Potomac's side;
Again the loon laughed mocking, and again
The echoes bayed far down the night and died,
While waking I recalled my wandering brain.

                              JAMES RUSSELL LOWELL.

BATTLE-HYMN OF THE REPUBLIC.

Nov.,
1861.

This war-song was written to the tune of "John Brown's Body," — a tune to which many thousands of Volunteers were marching to the front.

MINE eyes have seen the glory of the coming of
    the Lord:
He is trampling out the vintage where the grapes of
    wrath are stored;
He hath loosed the fateful lightning of His terrible
    swift sword:
        His truth is marching on.

I have seen Him in the watch-fires of a hundred circ-
    ling camps;
They have builded Him an altar in the evening dews
    and damps;
I can read His righteous sentence by the dim and flar-
    ing lamps.
        His day is marching on.

I have read a fiery gospel, writ in burnished rows of
    steel :
"As ye deal with My contemners, so with you My
    grace shall deal;
Let the Hero, born of woman, crush the serpent with
    His heel,
          Since God is marching on."

He has sounded forth the trumpet that shall never
    call retreat ;
He is sifting out the hearts of men before His judg-
    ment-seat :
Oh ! be swift, my soul, to answer Him ! be jubilant,
    my feet !
          Our God is marching on.

In the beauty of the lilies Christ was born across the sea,
With a glory in His bosom that transfigures you and me :
As He died to make men holy, let us die to make men
    free,
          While God is marching on.
                JULIA WARD HOWE.

AT PORT ROYAL.

1861.

THE tent-lights glimmer on the land,
  The ship-lights on the sea;
The night-wind smooths with drifting sand
  Our track on lone Tybee.

At last our grating keels outslide,
  Our good boats forward swing;
And while we ride the land-locked tide,
  Our negroes row and sing.

For dear the bondman holds his gifts
  Of music and of song:
The gold that kindly Nature sifts
  Among his sands of wrong;

The power to make his toiling days
  And poor home-comforts please;

The quaint relief of mirth that plays
  With sorrow's minor keys.

Another glow than sunset's fire
  Has filled the West with light,
Where field and garner, barn and byre,
  Are blazing through the night.

The land is wild with fear and hate,
  The rout runs mad and fast;
From hand to hand, from gate to gate,
  The flaming brand is passed.

The lurid glow falls strong across
  Dark faces broad with smiles;
Not theirs the terror, hate, and loss
  That fire yon blazing piles.

With oar-strokes timing to their song,
  They weave in simple lays
The pathos of remembered wrong,
  The hope of better days, —

The triumph-note that Miriam sung,
  The joy of uncaged birds:
Softening with Afric's mellow tongue
  Their broken Saxon words.

SONG OF THE NEGRO BOATMEN.

O, Praise an' tanks! De Lord he come
  To set de people free;
An' massa tink it day ob doom,
  An' we ob jubilee.
De Lord dat heap de Red Sea waves
  He jus' as 'trong as den;
He say de word: we las' night slaves;
  To-day, de Lord's freemen.
    De yam will grow, de cotton blow,
      We 'll hab de rice an' corn:
    O nebber you fear, if nebber you hear
      De driver blow his horn!

Ole massa on he trabbels gone;
  He leaf de land behind:

De Lord's breff blow him furder on,
  Like corn-shuck in de wind.
We own de hoe, we own de plough,
  We own de hands dat hold;
We sell de pig, we sell de cow,
  But nebber chile be sold.
    De yam will grow, de cotton blow,
      We 'll hab de rice an' corn:
    O nebber you fear, if nebber you hear
      De driver blow his horn!

We pray de Lord: he gib us signs
  Dat some day we be free;
De norf-wind tell it to de pines,
  De wild-duck to de sea;
We tink it when de church-bell ring,
  We dream it in de dream;
De rice-bird mean it when he sing,
  De eagle when he scream.
    De yam will grow, de cotton blow,
      We 'll hab de rice an' corn:

O nebber you fear, if nebber you hear
De driver blow his horn!

We know de promise nebber fail,
  An' nebber lie de word;
So like de 'postles in de jail,
  We waited for de Lord:
An' now he open ebery door
  An' trow away de key;
He tink we lub him so before,
  We lub him better free.
    De yam will grow, de cotton blow,
      He 'll gib de rice an' corn:
    O nebber you fear, if nebber you hear
      De driver blow his horn!

So sing our dusky gondoliers;
  And with a secret pain,
And smiles that seem akin to tears,
  We hear the wild refrain.

We dare not share the negro's trust,
　　Nor yet his hope deny;
We only know that God is just,
　　And every wrong shall die.

Rude seems the song; each swarthy face,
　　Flame-lighted, ruder still:
We start to think that hapless race
　　Must shape our good or ill;

That laws of changeless justice bind
　　Oppressor with oppressed;
And, close as sin and suffering joined,
　　We march to Fate abreast.

Sing on, poor hearts! your chant shall be
　　Our sign of blight or bloom,—
The Vala-song of Liberty,
　　Or death-rune of our doom!

　　　　　　　　　JOHN GREENLEAF WHITTIER.

READY.

1861.

L OADED with gallant soldiers,
   A boat shot in to the land,
And lay at the right of Rodman's Point,
   With her keel upon the sand.

Lightly, gayly, they came to shore,
   And never a man afraid;
When sudden the enemy opened fire
   From his deadly ambuscade.

Each man fell flat on the bottom
   Of the boat; and the captain said:
"If we lie here, we all are captured,
   And the first who moves is dead!"

Then out spoke a negro sailor,
   No slavish soul had he;

" Somebody 's got to die, boys,
   And it might as well be me !"

Firmly he rose, and fearlessly
   Stepped out into the tide ;
He pushed the vessel safely off,
   Then fell across her side :

Fell, pierced by a dozen bullets,
   As the boat swung clear and free ; —
But there was n't a man of them that day
   Who was fitter to die than he !

PHŒBE CAREY.

THE BRAVE AT HOME.

April 12,
   1861, — Fort Sumter.
April 9,
   1865, — Appomattox.

THE maid who binds her warrior's sash
    With smile that well her pain dissembles,
The while beneath her drooping lash
    One starry tear-drop hangs and trembles,
Though Heaven alone records the tear,
    And Fame shall never know her story,
Her heart has shed a drop as dear
    As e'er bedewed the field of glory!

The wife who girds her husband's sword,
    Mid little ones who weep or wonder,
And bravely speaks the cheering word,
    What though her heart be rent asunder,
Doomed nightly in her dreams to hear
    The bolts of death around him rattle,

Hath shed as sacred blood as e'er
  Was poured upon the field of battle!

The mother who conceals her grief
  While to her breast her son she presses,
Then breathes a few brave words and brief,
  Kissing the patriot brow she blesses,
With no one but her secret God
  To know the pain that weighs upon her,
Sheds holy blood as e'er the sod
  Received on Freedom's field of honor!

THOMAS BUCHANAN READ.

"HOW ARE YOU, SANITARY?"

1861—
1865. *Early in the war was organized the U. S. Sanitary
Commission, to supply comforts to the soldier in the
field from the voluntary contributions of the men and
women at home. Out of this grew the Red-Cross
Associations of Europe.*

DOWN the picket-guarded lane
   Rolled the comfort-laden wain,
Cheered by shouts that shook the plain,
   Soldier-like and merry :
Phrases such as camps may teach,
Sàbre-cuts of Saxon speech,
Such as "Bully!" "Them 's the peach!"
   "Wade in, Sanitary!"

Right and left the caissons drew
As the car went lumbering through,
Quick succeeding in review
   Squadrons military;
Sunburnt men with beards like frieze,
Smooth-faced boys, and cries like these, —

"U. S. San. Com."   "That's the cheese!"
"Pass in, Sanitary!"

In such cheer it struggled on
Till the battle front was won,
Then the car, its journey done,
Lo! was stationary;
And where bullets whistling fly,
Came the sadder, fainter cry,
"Help us, brothers, ere we die, —
Save us, Sanitary!"

Such the work. The phantom flies,
Wrapped in battle clouds that rise;
But the brave — whose dying eyes,
Veiled and visionary,
See the jasper gates swung wide,
See the parted throng outside —
Hears the voice to those who ride:
"Pass in, Sanitary!"

BRET HARTE.

SONG OF THE SOLDIERS.

1861 –
1865.

COMRADES known in marches many,
   Comrades, tried in dangers many,
Comrades, bound by memories many,
     Brothers let us be.
Wounds or sickness may divide us,
Marching orders may divide us,
But whatever fate betide us,
     Brothers of the heart are we.

Comrades, known by faith the clearest,
Tried when death was near and nearest,
Bound we are by ties the dearest,
     Brothers evermore to be.
And, if spared, and growing older,
Shoulder still in line with shoulder,

And with hearts no thrill the colder,
　　Brothers ever we shall be.

By communion of the banner, —
Crimson, white, and starry banner, —
By the baptism of the banner,
　　Children of one Church are we.
Creed nor faction can divide us,
Race nor language can divide us.
Still, whatever fate betide us,
　　Children of the flag are we.

　　　　　　　　CHARLES G. HALPINE.

JONATHAN TO JOHN.

Jan. 6,
1862.

*This poetic effusion of Mr. Hosea Biglow was preceded
by the Idyl of the Bridge and the Monument, which
set forth another side of American feeling at the
British words and deeds consequent on the unauthor-
ized capture, by Commodore Wilkes, of the Trent, con-
veying to England two Confederate Commissioners.*

IT don't seem hardly right, John,
  When both my hands was full,
To stump me to a fight, John, —
  Your cousin, tu, John Bull!
    Ole Uncle S. sez he, " I guess
    We know it now," sez he,
" The lion's paw is all the law,
    Accordin' to J. B.,
    Thet 's fit for you an' me!"

You wonder why we 're hot, John?
  Your mark wuz on the guns,
The neutral guns, thet shot, John,
  Our brothers an' our sons:

Ole Uncle S. sez he, " I guess
There 's human blood," sez he,
" By fits an' starts, in Yankee hearts,
Though 't may surprise J. B.
More 'n it would you an' me."

Ef *I* turned mad dogs loose, John,
On *your* front-parlor stairs,
Would it jest meet your views, John,
To wait and sue their heirs?
Ole Uncle S. sez he, " I guess,
I only guess," sez he,
" Thet ef Vattel on *his* toes fell,
'T would kind o' rile J. B.,
Ez wal ez you an' me! "

Who made the law thet hurts, John,
Heads I win, — ditto tails?
" *J. B.*" was on his shirts, John,
Onless my memory fails,
Ole Uncle S. sez he, " I guess
(I 'm good at thet)," sez he,

"Thet sauce for goose ain't *jest* the juice
  For ganders with J. B.,
  No more than you or me!"

When your rights was our wrongs, John,
  You did n't stop for fuss, —
Britanny's trident prongs, John,
  Was good 'nough law for us.
    Ole Uncle S. sez he, "I guess,
    Though physic 's good," sez he,
"It does n't foller that he can swaller
  Prescriptions signed '*J. B.*,'
  Put up by you an' me!"

We own the ocean, tu, John:
  You mus' n' take it hard,
Ef we can't think with you, John,
  It 's jest your own back-yard.
    Ole Uncle S. sez he, "I guess,
    Ef *thet 's* his claim," sez he,
"The fencin'-stuff 'll cost enough

To bust up friend J. B.,
 Ez wal ez you an' me!"

Why talk so dreffle big, John,
 Of honor when it meant
You did n't care a fig, John,
 But jest for *ten per cent?*
  Ole Uncle S. sez he, "I guess
  He 's like the rest," sez he:
"When all is done, it 's number one
  Thet's nearest to J. B.,
  Ez wal ez you an' me!"

We give the critters back, John,
 Cos Abram thought 't was right;
It warn't your bullyin' clack, John,
 Provokin' us to fight.
  Ole Uncle S. sez he, "I guess
  We 've a hard row," sez he,
"To hoe jest now; but thet somehow,
  May happen to J. B.,
  Ez wal ez you an' me!"

We ain't so weak an' poor, John,
 With twenty million people,
An' close to every door, John,
 A school-house an' a steeple.
  Ole Uncle S. sez he, " I guess
  It is a fact," sez he,
" The surest plan to make a Man
  Is, think him so, J. B.,
  Ez much ez you or me ! "

Our folks believe in Law, John;
 An' it 's for her sake, now,
They 've left the ax an' saw, John,
 The anvil an' the plough.
  Ole Uncle S. sez he, " I guess,
  Ef 't warn't for law," sez he,
" There 'd be one shindy from here to Indy;
  An' thet don't suit J. B.
  (When 't ain't 'twixt you an' me !) "

We know we 've got a cause, John,
 Thet 's honest, just an' true;

We thought 't would win applause, John,
  Ef nowheres else, from you.
    Ole Uncle S. sez he, " I guess
    His love of right," sez he,
" Hangs by a rotten fibre o' cotton :
    There 's natur' in J. B.,
    Ez wal ez you an' me ! "

The South says, "*Poor folks down !*" John,
  An, "*All men up !*" say we, —
White, yaller, black, an' brown, John :
  Now which is your idee ?
    Ole Uncle S. sez he, " I guess,
    John preaches wal," sez he ;
" But, sermon thru, an' come to *du*,
    Why, there 's the old J. B.
    A crowdin' you an' me ! "

Shall it be love, or hate, John ?
  It 's you thet 's to decide ;
Ain't *your* bonds held by Fate, John,
  Like all the world's beside ?

Ole Uncle S. sez he, " I guess
Wise men forgive," sez he,
" But not forget; an' some time yet
  · Thet truth may strike J. B.,
Ez wal ez you an' me!"

God means to make this land, John,
  Clear thru, from sea to sea,
Believe an' understand, John,
  The *wuth* o' bein' free.
    Ole Uncle S. sez he, " I guess,
    God's price is high," sez he;
" But nothin' else than wut He sells
    Wears long, an' thet J. B.
    May larn, like you an' me!"

JAMES RUSSELL LOWELL.

THE CUMBERLAND.

March 8,
1862.

*The Cumberland was sunk by the iron-clad rebel ram
" Merrimac," going down with her colors flying, and
firing even as the water rose over the gunwale.*

A T anchor in Hampton Roads we lay,
  On board of the Cumberland, sloop-of-war;
And at times from the fortress across the bay
  The alarum of drums swept past,
  Or a bugle blast
From the camp on the shore.

Then far away to the south uprose
  A little feather of snow-white smoke,
And we knew that the iron ship of our foes
  Was steadily steering its course
  To try the force
Of our ribs of oak.

Down upon us heavily runs,
  Silent and sullen, the floating fort;

Then comes a puff of smoke from her guns,
    And leaps the terrible death,
    With fiery breath,
  From each open port.

We are not idle, but send her straight
  Defiance back in a full broadside!
As hail rebounds from a roof of slate,
    Rebounds our heavier hail
    From each iron scale
  Of the monster's hide.

"Strike your flag!" the rebel cries,
  In his arrogant old plantation strain.
"Never!" our gallant Morris replies;
    "It is better to sink than to yield!"
    And the whole air pealed
  With the cheers of our men.

Then, like a kraken huge and black,
  She crushed our ribs in her iron grasp!

Down went the Cumberland all a wrack,
　With a sudden shudder of death,
　And the cannon's breath
For her dying gasp.

Next morn, as the sun rose over the bay,
　Still floated our flag at the mainmast head.
Lord, how beautiful was Thy day!
　　Every waft of the air
　　Was a whisper of prayer,
　Or a dirge for the dead.

Ho! brave hearts that went down in the seas!
　Ye are at peace in the troubled stream;
Ho! brave land! with hearts like these,
　　Thy flag, that is rent in twain,
　　Shall be one again,
　And without a seam!

　　　　　　　HENRY WADSWORTH LONGFELLOW.

THE OLD SERGEANT.

After
April 6-7,
1862.
(Shiloh.)

*This poem first appeared in the carrier's address of the
Louisville Journal, January 1, 1863.*

"COME a little nearer, Doctor, — thank you — let
me take the cup:

Draw your chair up, — draw it closer, — just another
little sup!

May be you think I'm better; but I'm pretty well
used up, —

Doctor, you've done all you could do, but I'm just a
going up!

"Feel my pulse, sir, if you want to, but it ain't much
use to try" —

"Never say that," said the Surgeon, as he smothered
down a sigh;

171

" It will never do, old comrade, for a soldier to say
    die ! "
" What you *say* will make no difference, Doctor, when
    you come to die.

" Doctor, what has been the matter ? " " You were
    very faint, they say ;
You must try to get to sleep now." " Doctor, have I
    been away ? "
" Not that anybody knows of ! " " Doctor — Doctor,
    please to stay !
There is something I must tell you, and you wont
    have long to stay !

" I have got my marching orders, and I 'm ready now
    to go ;
Doctor, did you say I fainted ? — but it could n't ha'
    been so, —
For as sure as I 'm a Sergeant, and was wounded at
    Shiloh,
I 've this very night been back there, on the old field
    of Shiloh.

"This is all that I remember: The last time the
    Lighter came,
And the lights had all been lowered, and the noises
    much the same,
He had not been gone five minutes before something
    called my name :
'ORDERLY-SERGEANT — ROBERT BURTON ! ' — just that
    way it called my name.

"And I wondered who could call me so distinctly and
    so slow,
Knew it could n't be the Lighter, — he could not have
    spoken so;
And I tried to answer, 'Here, sir!' but I could n't
    make it go;
For I could n't move a muscle, and I could n't make it go!

"Then I thought: It 's all a nightmare, all a humbug
    and a bore ;
Just another foolish *grape-vine* * — and it wont come
    any more ;

              * Canard.

But it came, sir, notwithstanding, just the same way as
  before :
' ORDERLY-SERGEANT — ROBERT BURTON ! ' even plainer
  than before.

"That is all that I remember, till a sudden burst of
  light,
And I stood beside the River, where we stood that
  Sunday night,
Waiting to be ferried over to the dark bluffs opposite,
When the river was perdition and all hell was opposite !

" And the same old palpitation came again in all its
  power,
And I heard a Bugle sounding, as from some celestial
  Tower ;
And the same mysterious voice said : ' IT IS THE
  ELEVENTH HOUR !
ORDERLY-SERGEANT — ROBERT BURTON !— IT IS THE
  ELEVENTH HOUR ! '

" Doctor Austin! what *day* is this?" "It is Wednes-
  day night, you know."
"Yes, — to-morrow will be New Year's, and a right
  good time below!
What *time* is it, Doctor Austin?" "Nearly Twelve."
  "Then don't you go!
Can it be that all this happened — all this — not an
  hour ago!

" There was where the gun-boats opened on the dark,
  rebellious host;
And where Webster semicircled his last guns upon the
  Coast;
There were still the two log-houses, just the same, or
  else their ghost, —
And the same old transport took me over — or its ghost!

" And the old field lay before me all deserted far and
  wide;
There was where they fell on Prentiss, — there McCler-
  nand met the tide;

There was where stern Sherman rallied, and where
    Hurlburt's heroes died, —
Lower down, where Wallace charged them, and kept
    charging till he died.

"There was where Lew Wallace showed them he was
    of the canny kin,
There was where old Nelson thundered, and where
    Rousseau waded in;
There McCook sent 'em to breakfast, and we all began
    to win —
There was where the grape-shot took me, just as we
    began to win.

"Now, a shroud of snow and silence over everything
    was spread;
And but for this old blue mantle and the old hat on
    my head,
I should not have even doubted, to this moment, I
    was dead, —
For my footsteps were as silent as the snow upon the
    dead!

" Death and silence! — Death and silence! all around
    me as I sped!
And behold, a mighty TOWER, as if builded to the
    dead, —
To the Heaven of the heavens, lifted up its mighty
    head,
Till the Stars and Stripes of Heaven all seemed waving
    from its head!

" Round and mighty-based it towered — up into the
    infinite —
And I knew no mortal mason could have built a shaft
    so bright;
For it shone like solid sunshine; and a winding stair
    of light,
Wound around it and around it till it wound clear out
    of sight!

" And, behold, as I approached it — with a rapt and
    dazzled stare, —
Thinking that I saw old comrades just ascending the
    great Stair, —

12

Suddenly the solemn challenge broke of—'Halt!' and
    'Who goes there!'
'I'm a friend,' I said, 'if you are.'—'Then advance,
    sir, to the Stair!'

"I advanced!—That sentry, Doctor, was Elijah Bal-
    lantyne!—
First of all to fall on Monday, after we had formed
    the line:
'Welcome, my old Sergeant, welcome! Welcome by
    that counter-sign!'
And he pointed to the scar there, under this old cloak
    of mine!

"As he grasped my hand, I shuddered, thinking only
    of the grave;
But he smiled and pointed upward with a bright and
    bloodless glaive;
'That's the way, sir, to Head-quarters.'—'What Head-
    quarters?'—'Of the Brave!'
'But the great Tower?' 'That,' he answered, 'is the
    way, sir, of the Brave!'

"Then a sudden shame came o'er me, at his uniform
 of light;
At my own so old and tattered, and at his so new and
 bright;
'Ah!' said he, 'you have forgotten the New Uniform
 to-night, —
Hurry back, for you must be here at just twelve o'clock
 to-night!'

"And the next thing I remember, you were sitting there,
 and I —
Doctor — did you hear a footstep? Hark! — God
 bless you all! Good by!
Doctor, please to give my musket and my knapsack,
 when I die,
To my Son — my Son that 's coming, — he wont get
 here till I die!

"Tell him his old father blessed him as he never did
 before, —
And to carry that old musket" — Hark! a knock is
 at the door! —

"Till the Union" — See! it opens! — "Father! Father!
    speak once more!"

"*Bless you!*" — gasped the old gray Sergeant, and he
    lay and said no more!

                            FORCEYTHE WILLSON.

THE RIVER FIGHT.

April 24, 1862.

The Confederate batteries defending the lower Mississippi mounted one hundred and twenty guns. Farragut ran his squadron past them " under such a fire from them," he wrote, " as I imagine the world has never seen." Beyond the forts he met and destroyed a fleet of twenty steamers, four iron-clad rams, and many fire-rafts. Only one of his ships was sunk.

DO you know of the dreary land,
   If land such region may seem,
Where 't is neither sea nor strand,
Ocean nor good dry land,
   But the nightmare marsh of a dream —
Where the Mighty River his death-road takes,
'Mid pools and windings that coil like snakes,
(A hundred leagues of bayous and lakes,)
   To die in the great Gulf Stream?

No coast-line clear and true,
(Granite and deep sea blue,)

On that dismal shore you pass —
Surf-worn boulder nor sandy beach,
But ooze-flats as far as the eye can reach,
 With shallows of water-grass —
Reedy savannas, vast and dun,
Lying dead in the dim March sun —
Huge rotting trunks and roots that lie
Like the blackened bones of the Shapes gone by,
 And miles of sunken morass.

No lovely, delicate thing
 Of life o'er the waste is seen —
But the cayman couched by his weedy spring,
 And the pelican, bird unclean —
Or the buzzard, flapping with heavy wing
 Like an evil ghost, o'er the desolate scene.

Ah, many a weary day
With our Leader there we lay,
 In the sultry haze and smoke,
Tugging our ships o'er the bar —
Till the Spring was wasted far,

Till his brave heart almost broke —
For the sullen River seemed
As if our intent he dreamed —
  All his shallow mouths did spew and choke.

But, ere April fully past,
All ground over at last,
And we knew the die was cast —
Knew the day drew nigh
To dare to the end one stormy deed,
Might save the Land at her sorest need,
  Or on the old deck to die!

Anchored we lay — and, a morn the more,
  To his captains and all his men
Thus wrote our stout old Commodore —
  (He was n't Admiral then:)

GENERAL ORDERS.

"Send your to' gallant masts down,
  Rig in each flying jib-boom!

Clear all ahead for the loom
Of traitor fortress and town,
Of traitor fleet bearing down.

"In with your canvas high —
We shall want no sail to fly!
Topsail and foresail, spanker and jib,
(With the heart of oak in the oaken rib,)
Shall serve us to win or die!

"Trim every hull by the head,
(So shall you spare the lead,)
Lest, if she ground, your ship swing round,
Bows in-shore, for a wreck —
See your grapnels all clear, with pains,
And a solid kedge in your port main-chains,
With a whip to the main-yard —
Drop it, heavy and hard,
When you grapple a traitor deck!

"On forecastle and on poop
Mount guns, as best you may deem —

If possible, rouse them up,
  (For still you must bow the stream) —
Also hoist and secure with stops
Howitzers firmly in your tops,
  To fire on the foe abeam.

" Look well to your pumps and hose —
  Have water-tubs, fore and aft,
  For quenching flame in your craft,
    And the gun-crews' fiery thirst —
See planks with felt fitted close,
  To plug every shot-hole tight —
  Stand ready to meet the worst!
  For if I have reckoned aright,
They will serve us shot, both cold and hot,
  Freely enough, to-night.

" Mark well each signal I make —
(Our life-long service at stake,
  And honor that must not lag !)
Whate'er the peril and awe,

In the battle's fieriest flaw,
Let never one ship withdraw
 Till orders come from the Flag!"

Would you hear of the River Fight?
It was two, of a soft spring night —
 God's stars looked down on all,
And all was clear and bright
But the low fog's chilling breath —
Up the River of Death
 Sailed the Great Admiral.

On our high poop-deck he stood,
 And round him ranged the men
Who have made their birthright good
 Of manhood, once and agen —
Lords of helm and of sail,
Tried in tempest and gale,
 Bronzed in battle and wreck —
Bell and Bailey grandly led
Each his Line of the Blue and Red —

Wainwright stood by our starboard rail,
  Thornton fought the deck.

And I mind me of more than they,
  Of the youthful, steadfast ones,
  That have shown them worthy sons
Of the Seamen passed away —
(Tyson conned our helm, that day,
  Watson stood by his guns.)

What thought our Admiral, then,
Looking down on his men?
  Since the terrible day,
    (Day of renown and tears!)
  When at anchor the Essex lay,
  Holding her foes at bay,
When, a boy, by Porter's side he stood
Till deck and plank-shear were dyed with blood,
    'T is half a hundred years —
  Half a hundred years, to-day!

Who could fail, with him?
Who reckon of life or limb?
  Not a pulse but beat the higher!
There had you seen, by the star-light dim,
Five hundred faces strong and grim —
  The Flag is going under fire!
Right up by the fort, with her helm hard a-port,
  The Hartford is going under fire!

The way to our work was plain,
Caldwell had broken the chain,
(Two hulks swung down amain,
  Soon as 't was sundered) —
Under the night's dark blue,
Steering steady and true,
Ship after ship went through —
Till, as we hove in view,
  Jackson out-thundered.

Back echoed Philip! ah, then —
Could you have seen our men,
  How they sprung, in the dim night haze,

To their work of toil and of clamor!
How the loaders, with sponge and rammer,
And their captains, with cord and hammer,
  Kept every muzzle ablaze!
How the guns, as with cheer and shout
Our tackle-men hurled them out,
  Brought up on the water-ways!

First, as we fired at their flash,
  'T was lightning and black eclipse,
With a bellowing roll and crash —
But soon, upon either bow,
  What with forts, and fire-rafts, and ships —
(The whole fleet was hard at it, now,
All pounding away!) — and Porter
Still thundering with shell and mortar —
  'T was the mighty sound and form
  Of an Equatorial Storm!

(Such you see in the Far South,
After long heat and drought,
  As day draws nigh to even —

Arching from North to South,
  Blinding the tropic sun,
  The great black bow comes on —
Till the thunder-veil is riven,
When all is crash and levin,
And the cannonade of heaven
  Rolls down the Amazon!)

But, as we worked along higher,
  Just where the river enlarges,
Down came a pyramid of fire —
  It was one of your long coal barges.
  (We had often had the like before) —
'T was coming down on us to larboard,
  Well in with the eastern shore —
  And our pilot, to let it pass round
  (You may guess we never stopped to sound,)
Giving us a rank sheer to starboard,
  Ran the Flag hard and fast aground!

'T was nigh abreast of the Upper Fort,
  And straightway a rascal Ram

(She was shaped like the devil's dam)
Puffed away for us, with a snort,
  And shoved it, with spiteful strength,
Right alongside of us, to port —
  It was all of our ship's length,
A huge crackling Cradle of the Pit!
  Pitch-pine knots to the brim,
  Belching flame red and grim —
What a roar came up from it!

Well, for a little it looked bad —
  But these things are, somehow, shorter
In the acting than the telling —
There was no singing-out nor yelling,
Nor any fussing and fretting,
  No stampede, in short —
But there we were, my lad,
  All a-fire on our port quarter!
Hammocks a-blaze in the netting,
  Flame spouting in at every port —
Our Fourth Cutter burning at the davit,
(No chance to lower away and save it.)

In a twinkling, the flames had risen
Halfway to main top and mizzen,
  Darting up the shrouds like snakes!
  Ah, how we clanked at the brakes,
  And the deep steam-pumps throbbed under,
  Sending a ceaseless flow —
Our top-men, a dauntless crowd,
Swarmed in rigging and shroud —
    There, ('t was a wonder!)
The burning ratlins and strands
They quenched with their bare hard hands —
    But the great guns below
    Never silenced their thunder!

At last, by backing and sounding,
When we were clear of grounding,
  And under head-way once more,
The whole rebel fleet came rounding
  The point —— if we had it hot before,
  'T was now, from shore to shore,
  One long, loud thundering roar —

Such crashing, splintering, and pounding,
  And smashing as you never heard before!

But that we fought foul wrong to wreck,
  And to save the Land we loved so well,
You might have deemed our long gun deck
  Two hundred feet of hell!

For all above was battle,
Broadside, and blaze, and rattle,
  Smoke and thunder alone —
(But, down in the sick-bay,
Where our wounded and dying lay,
  There was scarce a sob or a moan.)
And at last, when the dim day broke,
And the sullen sun awoke,
  Drearily blinking
O'er the haze and the cannon-smoke,
  That ever such morning dulls —
  There were thirteen traitor hulls
On fire and sinking!

13

Now, up the river! — though mad Chalmette
Sputters a vain resistance yet.
Small helm we gave her, our course to steer —
   'T was nicer work than you well would dream,
With cant and sheer to keep her clear
   Of the burning wrecks that cumbered the stream.

The Louisiana, hurled on high,
Mounts in thunder to meet the sky!
Then down to the depths of the turbid flood,
Fifty fathom of rebel mud!
The Mississippi comes floating down,
A mighty bonfire, from off the town —
And along the river, on stocks and ways,
A half-hatched devil's brood is a-blaze —
The great Anglo-Norman is all in flames,
(Hark to the roar of her tumbling frames!)
And the smaller fry that Treason would spawn,
Are lighting Algiers like an angry dawn!

From stem to stern, how the pirates burn,
   Fired by the furious hands that built!

So to ashes forever turn
  The suicide wrecks of wrong and guilt!

But as we neared the city,
  By field and vast plantation,
  (Ah, millstone of our Nation!)
With wonder and with pity
  What crowds we there espied
Of dark and wistful faces,
Mute in their toiling-places,
  Strangely and sadly eyed —
  Haply, 'mid doubt and fear,
  Deeming deliverance near —
  (One gave the ghost of a cheer!)

And on that dolorous strand,
  To greet the victor-brave
  One flag did welcome wave —
Raised, ah me! by a wretched hand
All outworn on our cruel Land, —
  The withered hand of a slave!

But all along the Levee,
  In a dark and drenching rain,
(By this, 't was pouring heavy,)
  Stood a fierce and sullen train —

A strange and a frenzied time!
  There were scowling rage and pain,
    Curses, howls, and hisses,
    Out of hate's black abysses —
Their courage and their crime
  All in vain — all in vain!

For from the hour that the Rebel Stream,
With the Crescent City lying abeam,
  Shuddered under our keel,
Smit to the heart with self-struck sting,
Slavery died in her scorpion-ring,
  And Murder fell on his steel.

'T is well to do and dare —
But ever may grateful prayer

Follow, as aye it ought,
When the good fight is fought,
  When the true deed is done —
Aloft in heaven's pure light,
(Deep azure crossed on white)
Our fair Church-Pennant waves
O'er a thousand thankful braves,
  Bareheaded in God's bright sun.

Lord of mercy and frown,
  Ruling o'er sea and shore,
  Send us such scene once more!
  All in Line of Battle
When the black ships bear down
On tyrant fort and town,
  'Mid cannon cloud and rattle —
  And the great guns once more
  Thunder back the roar
  Of the traitor walls ashore,
And the traitor flags come down!

HENRY HOWARD BROWNELL.

KEARNY AT SEVEN PINES.

May 31,
1862.

SO that soldierly legend is still on its journey, —
   That story of Kearny who knew not to yield!
'T was the day when with Jameson, fierce Berry, and
     Birney,
   Against twenty thousand he rallied the field,
Where the red volleys poured, where the clamor rose
     highest,
   Where the dead lay in clumps through the dwarf oak
     and pine,
Where the aim from the thicket was surest and
     nighest, —
   No charge like Phil Kearny's along the whole line.

When the battle went ill, and the bravest were solemn,
   Near the dark Seven Pines, where we still held our
     ground,

He rode down the length of the withering column,
   And his heart at our war-cry leapt up with a bound;
He snuffed, like his charger, the wind of our powder,—
   His sword waved us on and we answered the sign:
Loud our cheer as we rushed, but his laugh rang the
      louder,
   "There 's the devil's own fun, boys, along the whole
      line!"

How he strode his brown steed! How we saw his
      blade brighten
   In the one hand still left,— and the reins in his teeth!
He laughed like a boy when the holidays heighten,
   But a soldier's glance shot from his visor beneath.
Up came the reserves to the mellay infernal,
   Asking where to go in,— through the clearing or pine?
"O, anywhere! Forward! 'T is all the same, Colonel:
   You 'll find lovely fighting along the whole line!"

O, evil the black shroud of night at Chantilly,
   That hid him from sight of his brave men and tried!

Foul, foul sped the bullet that clipped the white lily,
  The flower of our knighthood, the whole army's pride!
Yet we dream that he still, — in that shadowy region
  Where the dead form their ranks at the wan drum-
      mer's sign, —
Rides on, as of old, down the length of his legion,
  And the word still is Forward! along the whole line.
                    EDMUND CLARENCE STEDMAN.

AFTER ALL.

May 31,
1862.

THE apples are ripe in the orchard,
  The work of the reaper is done,
And the golden woodlands redden
  In the blood of the dying sun.

At the cottage-door the grandsire
  Sits, pale, in his easy-chair,
While a gentle wind of twilight
  Plays with his silver hair.

A woman is kneeling beside him;
  A fair young head is prest,
In the first wild passion of sorrow,
  Against his aged breast.

And far from over the distance
  The faltering echoes come,

Of the flying blast of trumpet,
　And the rattling roll of drum.

And the grandsire speaks in a whisper,
　" The end no man can see;
But we give him to his country,
　And we give our prayers to Thee " . . . .

The violets star the meadows,
　The rose-buds fringe the door,
And over the grassy orchard
　The pink-white blossoms pour.

But the grandsire's chair is empty,
　The cottage is dark and still,
There 's a nameless grave in the battle-field,
　And a new one under the hill.

And a pallid, tearless woman
　By the cold hearth sits alone,
And the old clock in the corner
　Ticks on with a steady drone.

WILLIAM WINTER.

DIRGE FOR A SOLDIER.

Sept. 1, 1862.

These verses were written in memory of General Philip Kearny, killed at Chantilly after he had ridden out in advance of his men to reconnoitre.

CLOSE his eyes; his work is done!
   What to him is friend or foeman,
Rise of moon, or set of sun,
   Hand of man, or kiss of woman?
      Lay him low, lay him low,
      In the clover or the snow!
      What cares he? he can not know:
      Lay him low!

As man may, he fought his fight,
   Proved his truth by his endeavor;
Let him sleep in solemn night,
   Sleep forever and forever.
      Lay him low, lay him low,
      In the clover or the snow!

203

What cares he? he can not know:
Lay him low!

Fold him in his country's stars,
    Roll the drum and fire the volley!
What to him are all our wars,
    What but death bemocking folly?
        Lay him low, lay him low,
        In the clover or the snow!
        What cares he? he can not know:
        Lay him low!

Leave him to God's watching eye,
    Trust him to the hand that made him.
Mortal love weeps idly by:
    God alone has power to aid him,
        Lay him low, lay him low,
      · In the clover or the snow!
        What cares he? he can not know:
        Lay him low!

                    George H. Boker.

BARBARA FRIETCHIE.

Sept. **6,**
1862.

UP from the meadows rich with corn,
Clear in the cool September morn.

The clustered spires of Frederick stand
Green-walled by the hills of Maryland.

Round about them orchards sweep,
Apple and peach tree fruited deep,

Fair as a garden of the Lord
To the eyes of the famished rebel horde,

On that pleasant morn of the early fall,
When Lee marched over the mountain-wall,—

Over the mountains winding down,
Horse and foot, into Frederick town.

Forty flags with their silver stars,
Forty flags with their crimson bars,

Flapped in the morning wind: the sun
Of noon looked down, and saw not one.

Up rose old Barbara Frietchie then,
Bowed with her fourscore years and ten;

Bravest of all in Frederick town,
She took up the flag the men hauled down;

In her attic window the staff she set,
To show that one heart was loyal yet.

Up the street came the rebel tread,
Stonewall Jackson riding ahead.

Under his slouched hat left and right
He glanced; the old flag met his sight.

" Halt!" — the dust-brown ranks stood fast.
" Fire!" — out blazed the rifle-blast.

It shivered the window, pane and sash;
It rent the banner with seam and gash.

Quick, as it fell, from the broken staff
Dame Barbara snatched the silken scarf;

She leaned far out on the window-sill,
And shook it forth with a royal will.

"Shoot, if you must, this old gray head,
But spare your country's flag," she said.

A shade of sadness, a blush of shame,
Over the face of the leader came;

The nobler nature within him stirred
To life at that woman's deed and word:

"Who touches a hair of yon gray head
Dies like a dog! March on!" he said.

All day long through Frederick street
Sounded the tread of marching feet:

All day long that free flag tost
Over the heads of the rebel host.

Ever its torn folds rose and fell
On the loyal winds that loved it well;

And through the hill-gaps sunset light
Shone over it with a warm good-night.

Barbara Frietchie's work is o'er,
And the Rebel rides on his raids no more.

Honor to her! and let a tear
Fall, for her sake, on Stonewall's bier.

Over Barbara Frietchie's grave,
Flag of Freedom and Union, wave!

Peace and order and beauty draw
Round thy symbol of light and law;

And ever the stars above look down
On thy stars below in Frederick town!

JOHN GREENLEAF WHITTIER.

FREDERICKSBURG.

Dec. 13,
1862.

THE increasing moonlight drifts across my bed,
And on the churchyard by the road, I know
It falls as white and noiselessly as snow.
'T was such a night two weary summers fled;
The stars, as now, were waning overhead.
Listen! Again the shrill-lipped bugles blow
Where the swift currents of the river flow
Past Fredericksburg: far off the heavens are red
With sudden conflagration: on yon height,
Linstock in hand, the gunners hold their breath:
A signal-rocket pierces the dense night,
Flings its spent stars upon the town beneath:
Hark! — the artillery massing on the right,
Hark! — the black squadrons wheeling down to Death!

THOMAS BAILEY ALDRICH.

MUSIC IN CAMP.

Dec. 15–31,
1862.

TWO armies covered hill and plain
   Where Rappahannock's waters
Ran deeply crimsoned with the stain
   Of battle's recent slaughters.

The summer clouds lay pitched like tents
   In meads of heavenly azure;
And each dread gun of the elements
   Slept in its hid embrasure.

The breeze so softly blew, it made
   No forest leaf to quiver,
And the smoke of the random cannonade
   Rolled slowly from the river.

And now where circling hills looked down
   With cannon grimly planted,

O'er listless camp and silent town
  The golden sunset slanted;

When on the fervid air there came
  A strain, now rich, now tender,
The music seemed itself aflame
  With day's departing splendor.

A Federal band, which eve and morn
  Played measures brave and nimble,
Had just struck up with flute and horn
  And lively clash of cymbal.

Down flocked the soldiers to the bank;
  Till margined by its pebbles,
One wooded shore was blue with " Yanks,"
  And one was gray with " Rebels."

Then all was still; and then the band
  With movements light and tricksy,
Made stream and forest, hill and strand,
  Reverberate with " Dixie."

The conscious stream, with burnished glow,
  Went proudly o'er its pebbles,
But thrilled throughout its deepest flow
  With yelling of the Rebels.

Again a pause, and then again
  The trumpet pealed sonorous,
And Yankee Doodle was the strain
  To which the shore gave chorus.

The laughing ripple shoreward flew
  To kiss the shining pebbles —
Loud shrieked the crowding Boys in Blue
  Defiance to the Rebels.

And yet once more the bugle sang
  Above the stormy riot:
No shout upon the evening rang
  There reigned a holy quiet.

The sad, lone stream its noiseless tread
  Spread o'er the glistening pebbles:

All silent now the Yankees stood;
  All silent stood the Rebels:

For each responsive soul had heard
  That plaintive note's appealing,
So deeply " Home, Sweet Home " had stirred
  The hidden founts of feeling.

Or blue or gray, the soldier sees,
  As by the wand of fairy,
The cottage neath the live-oak trees,
  The cottage by the prairie.

Or cold or warm, his native skies
  Bend in their beauty o'er him:
Sending the tear-mist in his eyes —
  The dear ones stand before him.

As fades the iris after rain
  In April's tearful weather,
The vision vanished as the strain
  And daylight died together.

But memory, waked by music's art
  Expressed in simplest numbers,
Subdued the sternest Yankee's heart,
  Made light the Rebel's slumbers.

And fair the form of Music shines,
  That bright, celestial creature,
Who still 'mid war's embattled lines
  Gave this one touch of nature.

                    JOHN R. THOMPSON.

KEENAN'S CHARGE.

May 2, 1863.

During the second day of the battle of Chancellorsville, General Pleasonton was trying to get twenty-two guns into a vital position as Stonewall Jackson made a sudden advance. Time had to be bought; so Pleasanton ordered Major Peter Keenan, commanding the Eighth Pennsylvania Cavalry (four hundred strong), to charge the advancing ten thousand of the enemy. An introduction to the poem, setting forth these facts, is omitted.

BY the shrouded gleam of the western skies,
　Brave Keenan looked in Pleasonton's eyes
For an instant — clear, and cool, and still;
Then, with a smile, he said: "I will."

"Cavalry, charge!" Not a man of them shrank.
Their sharp, full cheer, from rank on rank,
Rose joyously, with a willing breath —
Rose like a greeting hail to death.
Then forward they sprang, and spurred and clashed;
Shouted the officers, crimson-sash'd;

Rode well the men, each brave as his fellow,
In their faded coats of the blue and yellow;
And above in the air, with an instinct true,
Like a bird of war their pennon flew.

With clank of scabbards and thunder of steeds,
And blades that shine like sunlit reeds,
And strong brown faces bravely pale
For fear their proud attempt shall fail,
Three hundred Pennsylvanians close
On twice ten thousand gallant foes.

Line after line the troopers came
To the edge of the wood that was ring'd with flame;
Rode in and sabered and shot — and fell;
Nor came one back his wounds to tell.
And full in the midst rose Keenan, tall
In the gloom, like a martyr awaiting his fall,
While the circle-stroke of his saber, swung
'Round his head, like a halo there, luminous hung.
Line after line; ay, whole platoons,

Struck dead in their saddles, of brave dragoons
By the maddened horses were onward borne
And into the vortex flung, trampled and torn;
As Keenan fought with his men, side by side.

So they rode, till there were no more to ride.

But over them, lying there, shattered and mute,
What deep echo rolls? — 'T is a death salute
From the cannon in place; for, heroes, you braved
Your fate not in vain: the army was saved!

Over them now — year following year —
Over their graves, the pine-cones fall,
And the whip-poor-will chants his specter-call;
But they stir not again: they raise no cheer:
They have ceased. But their glory shall never cease,
Nor their light be quenched in the light of peace.
The rush of their charge is resounding still
That saved the army at Chancellorsville.

GEORGE PARSONS LATHROP.

THE BLACK REGIMENT.

May 27,
1863.

"The colored troops fought nobly" was a frequent phrase in war bulletins; never did they better deserve this praise than at Port Hudson.

DARK as the clouds of even,
  Ranked in the western heaven,
Waiting the breath that lifts
All the dread mass, and drifts
Tempest and falling brand
Over a ruined land; —
So still and orderly,
Arm to arm, knee to knee,
Waiting the great event,
Stands the black regiment.

Down the long dusky line
Teeth gleam and eyeballs shine;
And the bright bayonet,
Bristling and firmly set,
Flashed with a purpose grand,

Long ere the sharp command
Of the fierce rolling drum
Told them their time had come,
Told them what work was sent
For the black regiment

" Now," the flag-sergeant cried,
" Though death and hell betide,
Let the whole nation see
If we are fit to be
Free in this land; or bound
Down, like the whining hound, —
Bound with red stripes of pain
In our old chains again!"
O, what a shout there went
From the black regiment!

" Charge!" Trump and drum awoke,
Onward the bondmen broke;
Bayonet and sabre-stroke
Vainly opposed their rush.
Through the wild battle's crush,

With but one thought aflush,
Driving their lords like chaff,
In the guns' mouths they laugh;
Or at the slippery brands
Leaping with open hands,
Down they tear man and horse,
Down in their awful course;
Trampling with bloody heel
Over the crashing steel,
All their eyes forward bent,
Rushed the black regiment.

" Freedom!" their battle-cry, —
" Freedom! or leave to die!"
Ah! and they meant the word,
Not as with us 't is heard,
Not a mere party shout:
They gave their spirits out;
Trusted the end to God,
And on the gory sod
Rolled in triumphant blood.

Glad to strike one free blow,
Whether for weal or woe;
Glad to breathe one free breath,
Though on the lips of death.
Praying — alas! in vain! —
That they might fall again,
So they could once more see
That burst to liberty!
This was what "freedom" lent
To the black regiment.

Hundreds on hundreds fell;
But they are resting well;
Scourges and shackles strong
Never shall do them wrong.

O, to the living few,
Soldiers, be just and true!
Hail them as comrades tried;
Fight with them side by side;
Never, in field or tent,
Scorn the black regiment.

GEORGE H. BOKER.

JOHN BURNS OF GETTYSBURG.

July 1, 2, 3,
    1863.

HAVE you heard the story that gossips tell
    Of Burns of Gettysburg? — No? Ah, well:
Brief is the glory that hero earns,
Briefer the story of poor John Burns:
He was the fellow who won renown, —
The only man who did n't back down
When the rebels rode through his native town;
But held his own in the fight next day,
When all his townsfolk ran away.
That was in July, Sixty-three,
The very day that General Lee,
Flower of Southern chivalry,
Baffled and beaten, backward reeled
From a stubborn Meade and a barren field.
I might tell how but the day before
John Burns stood at his cottage door,

Looking down the village street,
Where, in the shade of his peaceful vine,
He heard the low of his gathered kine,
And felt their breath with incense sweet;
Or I might say, when the sunset burned
The old farm gable, he thought it turned
The milk that fell like a babbling flood
Into the milk-pail red as blood!
Or how he fancied the hum of bees
Were bullets buzzing among the trees.
But all such fanciful thoughts as these
Were strange to a practical man like Burns,
Who minded only his own concerns,
Troubled no more by fancies fine
Than one of his calm-eyed, long-tailed, kine, —
Quite old-fashioned and matter-of-fact,
Slow to argue, but quick to act.
That was the reason, as some folks say,
He fought so well on that terrible day.

And it was terrible. On the right
Raged for hours the heady fight,

Thundered the battery's double bass, —
Difficult music for men to face;
While on the left — where now the graves
Undulate like the living waves
That all that day unceasing swept
Up to the pits the Rebels kept —
Round shot ploughed the upland glades,
Sown with bullets, reaped with blades;
Shattered fences here and there
Tossed their splinters in the air;
The very trees were stripped and bare;
The barns that once held yellow grain
Were heaped with harvests of the slain;
The cattle bellowed on the plain,
The turkeys screamed with might and main,
And brooding barn-fowl left their rest
With strange shells bursting in each nest.

Just where the tide of battle turns,
Eréct and lonely stood old John Burns.
How do you think the man was dressed?
He wore an ancient long buff vest,

Yellow as saffron, — but his best;
And, buttoned over his manly breast,
Was a bright blue coat, with a rolling collar,
And large gilt buttons, — size of a dollar, —
With tails that the country-folk called " swaller."
He wore a broad-brimmed, bell-crowned hat,
White as the locks on which it sat.
Never had such a sight been seen
For forty years on the village green,
Since old John Burns was a country beau,
And went to the " quiltings " long ago.

Close at his elbows all that day,
Veterans of the Peninsula,
Sunburnt and bearded, charged away;
And striplings, downy of lip and chin, —
Clerks that the Home Guard mustered in, —
Glanced, as they passed, at the hat he wore,
Then at the rifle his right hand bore;
And hailed him, from out their youthful lore,
With scraps of a slangy *répertoire:*

15

"How are you, White Hat?" "Put her through!"
"Your head's level!" and "Bully for you!"
Called him "Daddy," — begged he'd disclose
The name of the tailor who made his clothes,
And what was the value he set on those;
While Burns, unmindful of jeer and scoff,
Stood there picking the rebels off, —
With his long brown rifle and bell-crown hat,
And the swallow-tails they were laughing at.

'T was but a moment, for that respect
Which clothes all courage their voices checked;
And something the wildest could understand
Spake in the old man's strong right hand,
And his corded throat, and the lurking frown
Of his eyebrows under his old bell-crown;
Until, as they gazed, there crept an awe
Through the ranks in whispers, and some men saw, ,
In the antique vestments and long white hair,
The Past of the Nation in battle there;
And some of the soldiers since declare

That the gleam of his old white hat afar,
Like the crested plume of the brave Navarre,
That day was their oriflamme of war.

So raged the battle. You know the rest:
How the rebels, beaten and backward pressed,
Broke at the final charge, and ran.
At which John Burns — a practical man —
Shouldered his rifle, unbent his brows,
And then went back to his bees and cows.

That is the story of old John Burns;
This is the moral the reader learns:
In fighting the battle, the question 's whether
You 'll show a hat that 's white, or a feather!

BRET HARTE.

TWILIGHT ON SUMTER.

Aug. 24,
1863.

*After the surrender of Major Anderson, the Confederates
strengthened the fort; but, in the spring of 1863, the
U. S. guns on Morris Island battered it into a shapeless ruin.*

STILL and dark along the sea
  Sumter lay;
A light was overhead,
As from burning cities shed,
And the clouds were battle-red,
  Far away.
Not a solitary gun
Left to tell the fort had won,
  Or lost the day!
Nothing but the tattered rag
Of the drooping Rebel flag,
And the sea-birds screaming round it in their play.

How it woke one April morn,
    Fame shall tell;
As from Moultrie, close at hand,
And the batteries on the land,
Round its faint but fearless band
    Shot and shell
Raining hid the doubtful light;
But they fought the hopeless fight
    Long and well,
(Theirs the glory, ours the shame!)
Till the walls were wrapt in flame,
Then their flag was proudly struck, and Sumter fell!

    Now — oh, look at Sumter now,
      In the gloom!
Mark its scarred and shattered walls,
(Hark! the ruined rampart falls!)
There's a justice that appalls
      In its doom;
For this blasted spot of earth
Where Rebellion had its birth

Is its tomb!
And when Sumter sinks at last
From the heavens, that shrink aghast,
Hell shall rise in grim derision and make room!

RICHARD HENRY STODDARD.

NEW YEAR'S EVE.

Dec. 31,
1863.
Jan. 1,
1864.

Written in Libby Prison, Richmond.

'TIS twelve o'clock! Within my prison dreary,
  My head upon my hand, sitting so weary,
Scanning the future, musing on the past,
Pondering the fate that here my lot has cast,
The hoarse cry of the sentry on his beat
Wakens the echoes of the silent street, —

  "All 's well!"

Ah! is it so? My fellow-captive sleeping
Where the barred window strictest watch is keeping,
Dreaming of home and wife and prattling child,
Of the sequestered vale, the mountain wild, —
Tell me, when cruel morn shall break again,
Wilt thou repeat the sentinel's refrain,

  "All 's well!"

And thou, my country! Wounded, pale, and bleeding,
Thy children deaf to a fond mother's pleading,
Stabbing with cruel hate the nurturing breast
To which their infancy in love was prest, —
Recount thy wrongs, thy many sorrows name,
Then to the nations, if thou canst, proclaim,

" All 's well!"

But through the clouds the sun is slowly breaking;
Hope from her long deep sleep is re-awaking:
Speed the time, Father! when the bow of peace,
Spanning the gulf, shall bid the tempest cease,
When foemen, clasping each other by the hand,
Shall shout once more, in a united land,

" All 's well!"

F. A. BARTLESON.

THE BAY-FIGHT.

Aug. 5, 1864. *The poet was acting ensign on the staff of Admiral Far-ragut, when he led his squadron past Forts Morgan and Gaines, and into a victorious fight with the Con-federate fleet in the Bay of Mobile. The poem is here somewhat shortened.*

THREE days through sapphire seas we sailed,
  The steady Trade blew strong and free,
The Northern Light his banners paled,
The Ocean Stream our channels wet,
  We rounded low Canaveral's lee,
And passed the isles of emerald set
  In blue Bahama's turquoise sea.

By reef and shoal obscurely mapped,
  And hauntings of the gray sea-wolf,
The palmy Western Key lay lapped
  In the warm washing of the Gulf.

But weary to the hearts of all
  The burning glare, the barren reach

Of Santa Rosa's withered beach,
And Pensacola's ruined wall.

And weary was the long patrol,
   The thousand miles of shapeless strand,
From Brazos to San Blas that roll
   Their drifting dunes of desert sand.

Yet, coast-wise as 'we cruised or lay,
   The land-breeze still at nightfall bore,
By beach and fortress-guarded bay,
   Sweet odors from the enemy's shore,

Fresh from the forest solitudes,
   Unchallenged of his sentry lines —
The bursting of his cypress buds,
   And the warm fragrance of his pines.

Ah, never braver bark and crew,
   Nor bolder Flag a foe to dare.
Had left a wake on ocean blue
   Since Lion-Heart sailed *Trenc-le-mer!*

But little gain by that dark ground
 Was ours, save, sometime, freer breath
For friend or brother strangely found,
 'Scaped from the drear domain of death.

And little venture for the bold,
 Or laurel for our valiant Chief,
 Save some blockaded British thief,
Full fraught with murder in his hold,

Caught unawares at ebb or flood —
 Or dull bombardment, day by day,
 With fort and earth-work, far away,
Low couched in sullen leagues of mud.

A weary time, — but to the strong
 The day at last, as ever, came;
And the volcano, laid so long,
 Leaped forth in thunder and in flame!

  " Man your starboard battery ! "
  Kimberly shouted —

The ship, with her hearts of oak,
Was going, mid roar and smoke,
　　On to victory!
　　None of us doubted —
　　No, not our dying —
　　Farragut's flag was flying!

Gaines growled low on our left,
　　Morgan roared on our right —
Before us, gloomy and fell,
With breath like the fume of hell,
Lay the Dragon of iron shell,
　　Driven at last to the fight!

Ha, old ship! do they thrill,
　　The brave two hundred scars
　　You got in the River-Wars?
That were leeched with clamorous skill,
　　(Surgery savage and hard),
Splinted with bolt and beam,
Probed in scarfing and seam,

Rudely linted and tarred
With oakum and boiling pitch,
And sutured with splice and hitch,
  At the Brooklyn Navy-Yard!

Our lofty spars were down,
To bide the battle's frown
(Wont of old renown) —
But every ship was drest
In her bravest and· her best,
  As if for a July day;
Sixty flags and three,
  As we floated up the bay —
Every peak and mast-head flew
The brave Red, White, and Blue —
  We were eighteen ships that day.

With hawsers strong and taut,
The weaker lashed to port,
  On we sailed, two by two —
That if either a bolt should feel
Crash through caldron or wheel,

Fin of bronze or sinew of steel,
  Her mate might bear her through.

Steadily nearing the head,
The great Flag-Ship led,
  Grandest of sights!
On her lofty mizzen flew
Our Leader's dauntless Blue,
  That had waved o'er twenty fights —
So we went, with the first of the tide,
  Slowly, mid the roar
  Of the Rebel guns ashore
And the thunder of each full broadside.

Ah, how poor the prate
Of statute and state,
  We once held with these fellows —
Here, on the flood's pale-green,
  Hark how he bellows,
  Each bluff old Sea-Lawyer!
Talk to them, Dahlgren,
  Parrott, and Sawyer!

On, in the whirling shade
　Of the cannon's sulphury breath,
　We drew to the Line of Death
That our devilish Foe had laid —
Meshed in a horrible net,
　And baited villainous well,
Right in our path were set
　Three hundred traps of hell!

And there, O sight forlorn!
　There, while the cannon
　　Hurtled and thundered —
　(Ah, what ill raven
Flapped o'er the ship that morn!) —
Caught by the under-death,
In the drawing of a breath,
　Down went dauntless Craven,
　　He and his hundred!

A moment we saw her turret,
　A little heel she gave,
And a thin white spray went o'er her,

Like the crest of a breaking wave —
In that great iron coffin,
   The channel for their grave,
   The fort their monument,
(Seen afar in the offing,)
Ten fathom deep lie Craven,
   And the bravest of our brave.

Then, in that deadly track,
A little the ships held back,
   Closing up in their stations —
There are minutes that fix the fate
   Of battles and of nations
   (Christening the generations,)
When valor were all too late,
   If a moment's doubt be harbored
From the main-top, bold and brief,
Came the word of our grand old Chief —
   " Go on!" — 't was all he said —
   Our helm was put to the starboard,
      And the Hartford passed ahead.

Ahead lay the Tennessee,
　　On our starboard bow he lay,
With his mail-clad consorts three,
　　(The rest had run up the Bay) —
There he was, belching flame from his bow,
And the steam from his throat's abyss
Was a Dragon's maddened hiss —
　　In sooth a most cursèd craft! —
In a sullen ring at bay
By the Middle Ground they lay,
　　Raking us fore and aft.

　　Trust me, our berth was hot,
　　Ah, wickedly well they shot;
How their death-bolts howled and stung!
　　And the water-batteries played
　　With their deadly cannonade
Till the air around us rung;
So the battle raged and roared —
Ah, had you been aboard
　　To have seen the fight we made!
　　16

How they leaped, the tongues of flame,
From the cannon's fiery lip!
How the broadsides, deck and frame,
Shook the great ship!

And how the enemy's shell
Came crashing, heavy and oft,
Clouds of splinters flying aloft
And falling in oaken showers —
But ah, the pluck of the crew!
Had you stood on that deck of ours,
You had seen what men may do.

Still, as the fray grew louder,
Boldly they worked and well;
Steadily came the powder,
Steadily came the shell.
And if tackle or truck found hurt,
Quickly they cleared the wreck;
And the dead were laid to port,
All a-row, on our deck.

Never a nerve that failed,
Never a cheek that paled,
Not a tinge of gloom or pallor —
There was bold Kentucky's grit,
And the old Virginian valor,
And the daring Yankee wit.

There were blue eyes from turfy Shannon,
There were black orbs from palmy Niger —
But there, alongside the cannon,
Each man fought like a tiger!

A little, once, it looked ill,
Our consort began to burn —
They quenched the flames with a will,
But our men were falling still,
And still the fleet was astern.

Right abreast of the Fort
In an awful shroud they lay,
Broadsides thundering away,

And lightning from every port —
　Scene of glory and dread!

A storm-cloud all aglow
　With flashes of fiery red —
The thunder raging below,
　And the forest of flags o'erhead!

So grand the hurly and roar,
　So fiercely their broadsides blazed,
The regiments fighting ashore
　Forgot to fire as they gazed.

　There, to silence the Foe,
　Moving grimly and slow,
They loomed in that deadly wreath,
　Where the darkest batteries frowned —
　Death in the air all round,
And the black torpedoes·beneath!

And now, as we looked ahead,
　All for'ard, the long white deck

Was growing a strange dull red;
　But soon, as once and agen
Fore and aft we sped
　(The firing to guide or check,)
You could hardly choose but tread
　On the ghastly human wreck,
(Dreadful gobbet and shred
　　That a minute ago were men!)

Red, from mainmast to bitts!
　Red, on bulwark and wale —
Red, by combing and hatch —
　Red, o'er netting and rail!

And ever, with steady con,
　The ship forged slowly by —
And ever the crew fought on,
　And their cheers rang loud and high.

Grand was the sight to see
　　How by their guns they stood,
Right in front of our dead

Fighting square abreast —
Each brawny arm and chest
All spotted with black and red,
    Chrism of fire and blood!

Worth our watch, dull and sterile,
    Worth all the weary time —
Worth the woe and the peril,
    To stand in that strait sublime!

Fear?   A forgotten form!
    Death?   A dream of the eyes!
We were atoms in God's great storm
    That roared through the angry skies.

One only doubt was ours,
    One only dread we knew —
Could the day that dawned so well
Go down for the Darker Powers?
    Would the fleet get through?
    And ever the shot and shell
Came with the howl of hell,
The splinter-clouds rose and fell,

And the long line of corpses grew –
Would the fleet win through?

They are men that never will fail
  (How aforetime they 've fought!)
But Murder may yet prevail —
    They may sink as Craven sank.
  Therewith one hard, fierce thought,
Burning on heart and lip,
Ran like fire through the ship —
    Fight her, to the last plank!

A dimmer Renown might strike
  If Death lay square alongside —
But the Old Flag has no like,
  She must fight, whatever betide —
When the war is a tale of old,
And this day's story is told,
  They shall hear how the Hartford died!

But as we ranged ahead,
  And the leading ships worked in,
  Losing their hope to win,

The enemy turned and fled —
And one seeks a shallow reach,
  And another, winged in her flight,
  Our mate, brave Jouett, brings in —
  And one, all torn in the fight,
Runs for a wreck on the beach,
  Where her flames soon fire the night.

And the Ram, when well up the Bay,
  And we looked that our stems should meet,
(He had us fair for a prey,)
Shifting his helm midway,
  Sheered off and ran for the fleet;
There, without skulking or sham,
  He fought them, gun for gun,
And ever he sought to ram,
  But could finish never a one.

From the first of the iron shower
  Till we sent our parting shell,
'T was just one savage hour
  Of the roar and the rage of hell.

With the lessening smoke and thunder,
  Our glasses around we aim —
What is that burning yonder?
  Our Philippi, — aground and in flame!

Below, 't was still all a-roar,
As the ships went by the shore,
  But the fire of the fort had slacked,
(So fierce their volleys had been) —
And now, with a mighty din,
The whole fleet came grandly in,
  Though sorely battered and wracked.

So, up the Bay we ran,
  The Flag to port and ahead,
And a pitying rain began
  To wash the lips of our dead.

A league from the Fort we lay,
  And deemed that the end must lag;
When lo! looking down the Bay,
  There flaunted the Rebel Rag —

THE BAY-FIGHT.

The Ram is again under way,
  And heading dead for the Flag!

Steering up with the stream,
  Boldly his course he lay,
Though the fleet all answered his fire,
And, as he still drew nigher,
  Ever on bow and beam
    Our Monitors pounded away —
    How the Chickasaw hammered away!

Quickly breasting the wave,
  Eager the prize to win,
First of us all the brave
  Monongahela went in
Under full head of steam —
Twice she struck him abeam,
Till her stem was a sorry work,
  (She might have run on a crag!)
The Lackawanna hit fair,
He flung her aside like cork,
  And still he held for the Flag.

High in the mizzen shroud
  (Lest the smoke his sight o'erwhelm),
Our Admiral's. voice rang loud,
  " Hard-a-starboard your helm!
Starboard! and run him down!"
  Starboard it was — and so,
Like a black squall's lifting frown,
Our mighty bow bore down
  On the iron beak of the Foe.

We stood on the deck together,
  Men that had looked on death
In battle and stormy weather —
  Yet a little we held our breath,
  When, with the hush of death,
The great ships drew together.

Our Captain strode to the bow,
  Drayton, courtly and wise,
  Kindly cynic, and wise,

(You hardly had known him now, —
　The flame of fight in his eyes!)
His brave heart eager to feel
How the oak would tell on the steel!

But, as the space grew short,
　A little he seemed to shun us,
Out peered a form grim and lanky,
　And a voice yelled: "Hard-a-port!
Hard-a-port! — here 's the damned Yankee
　Coming right down on us!"

He sheered, but the ships ran foul;
With a gnarring shudder and growl —
　He gave us a deadly gun;
But as he passed in his pride,
(Rasping right alongside!)
　The Old Flag, in thunder tones,
Poured in her port broadside,
Rattling his iron hide,
　And cracking his timber bones!

Just then, at speed on the Foe,
  With her bow all weathered and brown,
  The great Lackawanna came down,
Full tilt, for another blow;
We were forging ahead,
  She reversed — but, for all our pains,
Rammed the old Hartford instead,
  Just for'ard the mizzen-chains!

Ah! how the masts did buckle and bend,
  And the stout hull ring and reel,
As she took us right on end!
  (Vain were engine and wheel,
  She was under full steam) —
With the roar of a thunder-stroke
Her two thousand tons of oak
  Brought up on us, right abeam!

A wreck, as it looked, we lay —
(Rib and plankshear gave way

To the stroke of that giant wedge!)
Here, after all, we go —
The old ship is gone! — ah, no,
    But cut to the water's edge.

Never mind then — at him again!
    His flurry now can't last long;
He 'll never again see land —
Try that on *him*, Marchand!
    On him again, brave Strong!

Heading square at the hulk,
    Full on his beam we bore;
But the spine of the huge Sea-Hog
Lay on the tide like a log,
    He vomited flame no more.

By this he had found it hot —
    Half the fleet, in an angry ring,
    Closed round the hideous Thing,
Hammering with solid shot,

And bearing down, bow on bow —
  He has but a minute to choose;
Life or renown ? — which now
  Will the Rebel Admiral lose ?

Cruel, haughty, and cold,
He ever was strong and bold —
  Shall he shrink from a wooden stem ?
He will think of that brave band
He sank in the Cumberland —
  Ay, he will sink like them.

Nothing left but to fight
Boldly his last sea-fight!
  Can he strike ?   By heaven, 't is true!
  Down comes the traitor Blue,
And up goes the captive White !

Up went the White! Ah then
The hurrahs that, once and agen,
Rang from three thousand men
  All flushed and savage with fight!

Our dead lay cold and stark,
But our dying, down in the dark,
Answered as best they might —
Lifting their poor lost arms,
And cheering for God and Right!

HENRY HOWARD BROWNELL.

SHERIDAN'S RIDE.

Oct. 19,
1864.

General Early surprised and routed the Union troops during General Sheridan's absence in Washington. Sheridan hastened to the front, rallied his men, and won a complete victory.

U P from the South at break of day,
    Bringing to Winchester fresh dismay,
The affrighted air with a shudder bore,
Like a herald in haste, to the chieftain's door,
The terrible grumble, and rumble, and roar, ·
Telling the battle was on once more,
And Sheridan twenty miles away.

And wider still those billows of war
Thundered along the horizon's bar;
And louder yet into Winchester rolled
The roar of that red sea uncontrolled,
Making the blood of the listener cold,
As he thought of the stake in that fiery fray,
And Sheridan twenty miles away.

But there is a road from Winchester town,
A good, broad highway leading down;
And there, through the flush of the morning light,
A steed as black as the steeds of night,
Was seen to pass, as with eagle flight,
As if he knew the terrible need;
He stretched away with his utmost speed;
Hills rose and fell; but his heart was gay,
With Sheridan fifteen miles away.

Still sprung from those swift hoofs, thundering South,
The dust, like smoke from the cannon's mouth;
Or the trail of a comet, sweeping faster and faster,
Foreboding to traitors the doom of disaster.
The heart of the steed and the heart of the master
Were beating like prisoners assaulting their walls,
Impatient to be where the battle-field calls;
Every nerve of the charger was strained to full play,
With Sheridan only ten miles away.

Under his spurning feet the road
Like an arrowy Alpine river flowed,

And the landscape sped away behind
Like an ocean flying before the wind,
And the steed, like a bark fed with furnace fire,
Swept on, with his wild eye full of ire.
But lo! he is nearing his heart's desire;
He is snuffing the smoke of the roaring fray,
With Sheridan only five miles away.

The first that the general saw were the groups
Of stragglers, and then the retreating troops,
What was done? what to do? a glance told him both,
Then striking his spurs, with a terrible oath,
He dashed down the line, mid a storm of huzzas,
And the wave of retreat checked its course there, because
The sight of the master compelled it to pause.
With foam and with dust, the black charger was gray
By the flash of his eye, and the red nostril's play,
He seemed to the whole great army to say,
" I have brought you Sheridan all the way
From Winchester, down to save the day! "

Hurrah! hurrah for Sheridan!
Hurrah! hurrah for horse and man!

And when their statues are placed on high,
Under the dome of the Union sky,
The American soldiers' Temple of Fame,
There with the glorious general's name
Be it said, in letters both bold and bright,
" Here is the steed that saved the day,
By carrying Sheridan into the fight,
From Winchester, twenty miles away!"

THOMAS BUCHANAN READ.

SHERMAN'S MARCH TO THE SEA.

May 4,
1864.
Dec. 21,
1864.

After Sherman left Tennessee in May, to the taking of Atlanta September 2d, there was hardly a day without its battle; after he left Atlanta he marched to the sea and took Savannah; then he went to Columbia and the backbone of the Rebellion was broken. The poet wrote this while a prisoner at Columbia; and when Sherman arrived there and read it, he attached Adjt. Byers to his staff.

OUR camp-fires shone bright on the mountain
 That frowned on the river below,
As we stood by our guns in the morning,
 - And eagerly watched for the foe;
When a rider came out of the darkness
 That hung over mountain and tree,
And shouted, "Boys, up and be ready!
 For Sherman will march to the sea!"

Then cheer upon cheer for bold Sherman
 Went up from each valley and glen,
And the bugles re-echoed the music
 That came from the lips of the men;

For we knew that the stars in our banner
  More bright in their splendor would be,
And that blessings from Northland would greet us,
  When Sherman marched down to the sea.

Then forward, boys! forward to battle!
  We marched on our wearisome way,
We stormed the wild hills of Resaca —
  God bless those who fell on that day!
Then Kenesaw, dark in its glory,
  Frowned down on the flag of the free;
But the East and the West bore our standard
  And Sherman marched down to the sea.

Still onward we pressed, till our banners
  Swept out from Atlanta's grim walls,
And the blood of the patriot dampened
  The soil where the traitor-flag falls;
We paused not to weep for the fallen,
  Who slept by each river and tree,
Yet we twined them a wreath of the laurel,
  As Sherman marched down to the sea.

Oh, proud was our army that morning,
   That stood where the pine darkly towers,
When Sherman said, " Boys, you are weary,
   But to-day fair Savannah is ours!"
Then sang we the song of our chieftain,
   That echoed o'er river and lea,
And the stars in our banner shone brighter
   When Sherman marched down to the sea.

              SAMUEL H. M. BYERS.

THE SONG OF SHERMAN'S ARMY.

Nov. 12, 1864. Dec. 21, 1864.

The march from Atlanta to Savannah was a joyous frolic in comparison with the hard work and hard fighting before and after it.

A PILLAR of fire by night,
  A pillar of smoke by day,
Some hours of march — then a halt to fight,
  And so we hold our way;
Some hours of march — then a halt to fight,
  As on we hold our way.

Over mountain and plain and stream,
  To some bright Atlantic bay,
With our arms aflash in the morning beam,
  We hold our festal way;
With our arms aflash in the morning beam,
  We hold our checkless way!

There is terror wherever we come,
  There is terror and wild dismay

When they see the Old Flag and hear the drum
    Announce us on the way;
When they see the Old Flag and hear the drum
    Beating time to our onward way.

    Never unlimber a gun
        For those villainous lines in gray,
Draw sabers! and at 'em upon the run!
        'T is thus we clear our way;
Draw sabers, and soon you will see them run,
    As we hold our conquering way.

    The loyal, who long have been dumb,
        Are loud in their cheers to-day;
And the old men out on their crutches come,
        To see us hold our way;
And the old men out on their crutches come,
    To bless us on our way.

    Around us in rear and flanks,
        Their futile squadrons play,
With a sixty-mile front of steady ranks,

We hold our checkless way;
With a sixty-mile front of serried ranks,
Our banner clears the way.

Hear the spattering fire that starts
From the woods and copses gray,
There is just enough fighting to quicken our hearts
As we frolic along the way!
There is just enough fighting to warm our hearts,
As we rattle along the way.

Upon different roads, abreast,
The heads of our columns gay,
With fluttering flags, all forward pressed,
Hold on their conquering way;
With fluttering flags to victory pressed,
We hold our glorious way.

Ah, traitors! who bragged so bold
In the sad war's early day,
Did nothing predict you should ever behold
The Old Flag come this way?

Did nothing predict you should yet behold
    Our banner come back this way?

    By heaven! 't is a gala march,
      'T is a pic-nic or a play;
Of all our long war 't is the crowning arch,
      Hip, hip! for Sherman's way!
Of all our long war this crowns the arch —
    For Sherman and Grant, hurrah!
                CHARLES G. HALPINE.

O CAPTAIN! MY CAPTAIN!

April 15,
1865.
*Abraham Lincoln was killed by John Wilkes Booth,
almost exactly four years after the first shot was
fired at Fort Sumter.*

O CAPTAIN! my Captain! our fearful trip is done;
   The ship has weather'd every rack, the prize
we sought is won;
The port is near, the bells I hear, the people all
   exulting,
While follow eyes the steady keel, the vessel grim and
   daring:
     But O heart! heart! heart!
      O the bleeding drops of red,
       Where on the deck my Captain lies,
        Fallen cold and dead!

O Captain! my Captain! rise up and hear the bells;
Rise up — for you the flag is flung — for you the
   bugle trills;

For you bouquets and ribbon'd wreaths — for you the
    shores a-crowding;
For you they call, the swaying mass, their eager faces
    turning;
      Here Captain! dear father! ·
       This arm beneath your head;
        It is some dream that on the deck
        You 've fallen cold and dead.

My Captain does not answer, his lips are pale and still;
My father does not feel my arm, he has no pulse nor
    will:
The ship is anchor'd safe and sound, its voyage closed
    and done;
From fearful trip the victor ship, comes in with object
    won:
      Exult, O shores, and ring, O bells!
       But I, with mournful tread,
        Walk the deck my Captain lies,
        Fallen cold and dead.

                  WALT WHITMAN.

ABRAHAM LINCOLN.

April 15,
1865.

This is a fragment of the noble Commemoration Ode delivered at Harvard College to the memory of those of its students who fell in the war which kept the country whole.

SUCH was he, our Martyr-Chief,
  Whom late the Nation he had led,
  With ashes on her head,
Wept with the passion of an angry grief:
Forgive me, if from present things I turn
To speak what in my heart will beat and burn,
And hang my wreath on his world-honored urn.
    Nature, they say, doth dote,
    And cannot make a man
    Save on some worn-out plan,
    Repeating us by rote:
For him her Old World moulds aside she threw,
  And, choosing sweet clay from the breast

Of the unexhausted West,
With stuff untainted shaped a hero new,
Wise, steadfast in the strength of God, and true.
How beautiful to see
Once more a shepherd of mankind indeed,
Who loved his charge, but never loved to lead;
One whose meek flock the people joyed to be,
Not lured by any cheat of birth,
But by his clear-grained human worth,
And brave old wisdom of sincerity!
They knew that outward grace is dust;
They could not choose but trust
In that sure-footed mind's unfaltering skill,
And supple-tempered will
That bent like perfect steel to spring again and thrust.
His was no lonely mountain-peak of mind,
Thrusting to thin air o'er our cloudy bars,
A sea-mark now, now lost in vapors blind;
Broad prairie rather, genial, level-lined,
Fruitful and friendly for all human kind,
Yet also nigh to heaven and loved of loftiest stars.

Nothing of Europe here,
Or, then, of Europe fronting mornward still,
Ere any names of Serf and Peer
Could Nature's equal scheme deface;
Here was a type of the true elder race,
And one of Plutarch's men talked with us face to face.

I praise him not; it were too late;
And some innative weakness there must be
In him who condescends to victory
Such as the Present gives, and cannot wait,
Safe in himself as in a fate.

So always firmly he:
He knew to bide his time,
And can his fame abide,
Still patient in his simple faith sublime,
Till the wise years decide.

Great captains, with their guns and drums,
Disturb our judgment for the hour,
But at last silence comes;
These all are gone, and, standing like a tower,
Our children shall behold his fame,

The kindly-earnest, brave, foreseeing man,
Sagacious, patient, dreading praise, not blame,
New birth of our new soil, the first American.

JAMES RUSSELL LOWELL.

18

THE BLUE AND THE GRAY.

1867. *The women of Columbus, Mississippi, had shown them-*
selves impartial in the offerings made to the memory
of the dead. They strewed flowers alike on the
graves of the Confederate and of the National
soldiers.

BY the flow of the inland river,
  Whence the fleets of iron have fled,
Where the blades of the grave-grass quiver,
  Asleep on the ranks of the dead;
    Under the sod and the dew,
      Waiting the judgment day;
    Under the one, the Blue;
      Under the other, the Gray.

These in the robings of glory,
  Those in the gloom of defeat;
All with the battle-blood gory,
  In the dusk of eternity meet;

Under the sod and the dew,
    Waiting the judgment day;
Under the laurel, the Blue;
    Under the willow, the Gray.

From the silence of sorrowful hours,
    The desolate mourners go,
Lovingly laden with flowers,
    Alike for the friend and the foe;
        Under the sod and the dew,
            Waiting the judgment day;
        Under the roses, the Blue;
            Under the lilies, the Gray.

So, with an equal splendor,
    The morning sun-rays fall,
With a touch impartially tender,
    On the blossoms blooming for all;
        Under the sod and the dew,
            Waiting the judgment day;
        Broidered with gold, the Blue;
            Mellowed with gold, the Gray.

So, when the summer calleth,
  On forest and field of grain,
With an equal murmur falleth
  The cooling drip of the rain;
    Under the sod and the dew,
      Waiting the judgment day;
    Wet with the rain, the Blue;
      Wet with the rain, the Gray.

Sadly, but not with upbraiding,
  The generous deed was done;
In the storm of the years that are fading,
  No braver battle was won;
    Under the sod and the dew,
      Waiting the judgment day;
    Under the blossoms, the Blue;
      Under the garlands, the Gray.

No more shall the war-cry sever,
  Or the winding rivers be red;
They banish our anger for ever,
  When they laurel the graves of our dead.

Under the sod and the dew,
　　Waiting the judgment day;
Love and tears for the Blue;
　　Tears and love for the Gray.

FRANCIS MILES FINCH.

THE SHIP OF STATE.

1776.
1876.

This fragment is the conclusion of the Building of the Ship.

THOU, too, sail on, O Ship of State!
    Sail on, O UNION, strong and great!
Humanity, with all its fears,
With all the hopes of future years,
Is hanging breathless on thy fate!
We know what Master laid thy keel,
What Workmen wrought thy ribs of steel,
Who made each mast, and sail, and rope,
What anvils rang, what hammers beat,
In what a forge and what a heat
Were shaped the anchors of thy hope!
Fear not each sudden sound and shock,
'T is of the wave and not the rock;
'T is but the flapping of the sail,
And not a rent made by the gale!

In spite of rock and tempest's roar,
In spite of false lights on the shore,
Sail on, nor fear to breast the sea!
 Our hearts, our hopes, are all with thee,
Our hearts, our hopes, our prayers, our tears,
Our faith triumphant o'er our fears,
Are all with thee, — are all with thee!

HENRY WADSWORTH LONGFELLOW.

TABLE OF AUTHORS.

www.ingramcontent.com/pod-product-compliance
Lightning Source LLC
Chambersburg PA
CBHW031410270326
41929CB00010BA/1397